" *'Getting Where You Need to Go' by Abe Brown is a must read – not just once, but repeatedly! This new book is extremely thought provoking and provides the reader with practical and real views on who you are and the life you could be living. Every day, people get caught up in their hectic lives doing what is 'expected' of them, feeling how others want them to feel and trying to figure 'things' out. During these times, if we are fortunate, someone or something comes along that causes us to 'take pause' and 'think' about what is really important; and, then to look at ways to evoke changes that can provide us with a much healthier and improved outlook on the life we are living. It makes us think about who we are, why we are here, are we truly living or do we just exist day by day, are we really doing our best and can we make changes. This book speaks to what most of us already know; however, our busy lives puts up road blocks or creates detours that causes us delays into what is really important – 'what is my purpose' and 'how do I figure out my purpose'. Abe has figured this out perfectly and shares realistic views on obtaining optimal living and making the most of who you are and provides realistic guidelines to self-discovery. If you are looking at discovering your inner self and aspiring to a greater and more fulfilling and happy life, then you must read this book!"*
Deborah J. Lohrenz, CIM, RPR, CMP, CCP
Recruitment Consultant, Bell Aliant Regional Communications

"Abe, I am super excited about your new book. It is going to make a big difference in the lives of anyone who wants to really get where they need to be. I have read hundreds of good self help books but I found myself taking notes from almost every page. You have created a very practical resource that offers a host of fresh insights into personal growth and life achievement. I would highly recommend your book, 'Getting Where You Need To Go' to those who really want to live 'a life that counts'. Great job!"
Larry Scarbeau, Life Mastery Coach,
My Crystal Clear Future Inc.
www.mycrystalclearfuture.com

"Abe applied a 21 Day L.I.F.E.F.I.T Roadmap to answering the BIG questions – 'Who am I, and what was I meant to do?' Despite Abe's own personal hardships, he made the healthy choices to transform and release his potential. Now, you can too!"

Shelley Cox, Certified Career and Life Management Coach

"Getting To Where You Need To Go" packs a wallop that I wasn't prepared for! It has an energy that builds momentum by demanding the reader's attention and focus, and delivering in return, wisdom, encouragement and inspiration. Abe Brown – like the Master Coach that he is – offers page after page of well-crafted strategies for the readers to discover the vital links between life, living, and purpose regardless of where they are in the life cycle. It's all here... strategically laid-out – step-by-step – like an imaginative Lego creation: a snapped-in, locked-in pathway for an invigorating journey. 'Getting To Where You Need To Go' is a book you want to learn!"

Gordon Colledge
Conference Speaker, Professional Mediator,
Certified Life Coach Practitioner

"This book is an absolute must-have for pushing past internal barriers, identifying your unique abilities and unleashing your true potential. Abe Brown couples an honest, self-reflective approach with a challenging call to action. It truly is a user's manual for living a passionate and successful life."

Erin-Brie Warwick, LLB, CPC, Warwick Life Strategies
www.warwicklifestrategies.com

"Abe's book is the Leprechaun of Life Coach books because it is focused on your pot of gold, fun to play with, and fits in your back pocket. Lovin' your 'lucky charms' Abe!"

Tyler Hayden, Motivational Keynote Speaker, Author,
Creator of Team Building Programs
www.tylerhayden.com

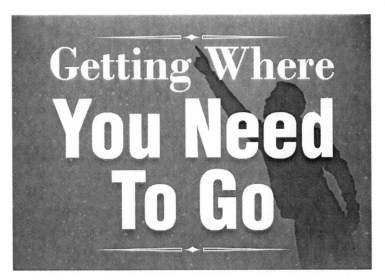

Getting Where You Need To Go

A Journey In Self-Discovery &

Living A Life That Counts

Abe Brown, B.Th., M.R.Ed./C.

Certified Master Coach Trainer

4

Cover design by Steven Lacey and Abe Brown.
Book design by Abe Brown and
Kathryn Marcellino, www.MarcellinoDesign.com

Abe Brown
Visit my website at www.MomentumCoaching.ca
www.CertifiedCoachesFederation.com

Printed in the United States of America

ISBN 978-0-9866913-0-0

Dedication

For my children,
Joshua David,
Julianna Joy

*When I am with you,
it is as close to heaven as I've ever been.*

And for my mom,
Mary Ellen.
I love you always.

And my brother,
Jason.
We will always be together, always be bros.

And my wife,
Leonisa.
*Babe I am grateful to God for you!
I love you!*

**"You Want To Be The Song,
Be The Song That You Hear In Your Head."**

"Discotheque" – U2 Song

Getting Where YOU Need To Go

Table Of Contents

Getting Where YOU Need To Go =
Living Your "L.I.F.E.F.I.T."

8

Acknowledgements

George Colman said, *"Praise the bridge that carried you over."* We have all been carried over and supported by many bridges throughout our lives. These bridges have acted to close the gap between where we are now, and where we want to go. Without them, we may never become all we can become. I am the product of all who have reached into my life, seen the good, and made me better. Thank you all so much!

I wish to thank all the mentors and coaches I have had. Some are listed in this book, and others are not.

Derrick Sweet, you've made a world of difference for me. You saw the good in me when few did, and you drew it out. Thank you.

Pastor Ted Yuke, you have been a consistent force for positive change in my life, and my life would be far less without you. You have enhanced and empowered who I am. Thanks.

Drs. George & Hazel Hill, you treated me like a son. I am eternally grateful. Thank you. Your coaching shaped me like no one else's.

Jason, Bruce and Evan, you guys rock!

George Brookman, you mentor and coach me, even if you don't know it. Your perspectives are unique and informed. Always passionate. Thank you.

Ron Silverstein, Kevin Parker, Adam Berube, Vibish Gurumurthi, James Heaver. Sandy MacDonald. You have all have made significant contributions in my professional life, and it is appreciated! You guys take passion and excellence to the next level. Thank you!

I want to thank those who have allowed me to lead, train, teach, and coach them – from students in the college and members of my churches in the past, to those who allow me to coach, mentor, and train them today. You have all taught me far more than I could ever teach you. I thank you, from my heart.

I wish to thank my family. Joshua and Julianna, you are my world. My life. All my hopes and dreams. My babe Euniz, thank you so much for your love and your support. I thank God for you every day as my Mahal. My brother Jason. My Mom and Don, and all my other family members. Family is always family. Love. Support. Strength. Prayer. I have received all of these and more. Thanks!

I want to thank my partners who helped me put this book together. Neil Everton, Steven Lacey, Kathryn Marcellino, and Lightning Source. Tyler Hayden, thank you for being a significant resource. Louise Burley, you inspired me more than you know. Thanks!

Lastly, I wish to thank some deep and long-time friends. We all get by, with a little help from our friends. Ron Swanson. Wow! What a deep connection and true friendship we've had. Sam Wolde-Michael. Yene guadegna! From the moment we met, you became my friend and my brother! Shell and Susan Clarke. Dan and Liz Reimer. Norm Sparks. Queen and Victor. Dean and Michele. Brad and Olivia. Rob and Mel. Troy Claridge. Jeff Brown. All my friends. Thank you all so much for standing with me, through it all.

Introduction – *The 21-Day Plan To Get You Going*

Who am I?

What am I?

Who and *What* am I supposed to be?

Why am I?

And *How* do I get the *Who*, the *What*, and the *Why* to flow together, or to flow at all?

The answers to these questions cut to the core and essence of what it means to be a whole, complete and fully functioning member of the human race. They draw us to a place of inner alignment, harmony, and personal contentment. These questions, and their answers, are the reason this book exists.

In the last 15+ years, I have had the pleasure and opportunity of working with people. For 7 years, I had the unique privilege of being the Academic Dean of a thriving post-secondary College located in beautiful Calgary, just east of the Rocky Mountains in Canada. In those 7 years, I sat down with literally hundreds of students and prospective students, one-on-one. During those 7 years, and in the 5 years that preceded them, I was also the Senior Pastor of two growing and vibrant churches. In that capacity, I had the opportunity to spend time one-on-one with hundreds of regular people. I have spent several years in business, rubbing shoulders with people of all walks of life. I am a Certified Master Coach and spend hours not only coaching others, but also training and certifying others to coach. And, somewhere in all of that, I was a part-time social worker for 11 years, devoting my time to helping the homeless with food and shelter, as well as life skills, coping with addictions, self-building, and career counselling.

In these times, if there is one thing I have discovered, it is that people thrive when they have a sense of purpose, and they wither and fade when they do not. Whether one is a person of faith or not, rich or poor, educated or uneducated, young or old, no matter what their ethnic background or race, male and female, whatever their personality type, we all desperately need a sense of purpose, a "life mission". Human beings are wired this way. When we discover why we were born, our personal "life mission", we flourish as we embrace life with a sense of destiny. But when we do not discover this, we wither away. As Benjamin Franklin said, *"Most people die at 25... but get buried at 75"*. The death happens when we live without a purpose; the burial, when our physical body expires. Charles Lamb said: *"Our spirits grow gray before our hair."* If we do not discover our "why" we quickly say, "Good-bye".

This need for a personal "life mission" is thoroughly documented. Dr. Viktor Frankl, the well-known psychologist, in his book, *The Search For Meaning[1]*, detailed how life in a Nazi death camp was made bearable only through this sense of hope, this sense of purpose; this sense of a personal "life mission". He later developed this concept into a well-known philosophy of psychotherapy called, *"Logotherapy"*. He taught that many perceived mental and emotional illnesses are in fact indicators or symptoms of a sense of having no purpose; a sense of meaninglessness and emptiness just below the surface of a person's life. Logotherapy aims to help eliminate that meaninglessness by helping the client to discover and develop his or her personal mission in life. As Nietzsche said, *"He who has a why to live for can bear with almost any how."*

My experience, from working with people, is that this is absolutely true! I have sat so many times in my office or in a coffee shop or in someone's home, counselling them through depression, discouragement, and despair, realizing that their underlying problem was not their job or their spouse or their finances or their children or their felt need; quite simply, they lacked a reason for getting out of bed each morning. When you lose your "Why?" you can say, "Good-Bye": *"Good-Bye"* to happiness, *"Good-Bye"* to fulfilment, *"Good-Bye"* to significance, *"Good-Bye"* to satisfaction!

---

[1] Frankl, Viktor E., *Man's Search for Meaning*, Washington Square Press, Simon and Schuster, New York, 1963

Success today has many definitions, and seems to some to be such an elusive destination with a hidden path. In this book, my urgent plea is to re-define success not so much as what you accumulate and accomplish, but as how closely you come to *Getting Where You Need To Go*. We all have somewhere we need to go specific to ourselves; different from the person in the office stall beside ours. There is a different melody playing within each of our souls... and "success" can rightly be defined as how closely our lives align with and express that melody. I love what Bono, the lead singer and writer of U2, said: *"I judge where we are by how close I am to the melody I'm hearing in my head, and how close are we to what we can do as a band to realizing our potential."* [2] True success is playing close to the melody... it is realizing our personal potential... it is *Getting Where You Need To Go. Getting Where You Need To Go* is all about your personal *"life mission"*: your **"L.I.F.E.F.I.T."**:

L – Learning About Your **Passions**

I – Investigating Your **Personality**

F – Finding Out Your **Gifts & Abilities**

E – Exploring & Clarifying Your **Mission**

F – Facilitating & Developing **Marketable Skills**

I – Including **Networking** & **Relationships**

T– Taking **Opportunities** As They Arise

In life and in serving, it's crucial that we Discover & Live Our **LIFEFIT**. We don't want to be stumbling around in the dark, wondering what to do and why we were born. We don't want to be stumbling around at all, as life and people and circumstances impose their will for us on us. Let's proactively engage life and *Get Where We Need To Go* BY discovering & living Our **LIFEFIT**. Then, we can confidently impose that upon life so that

[2] Assayas, Michka, *Bono In Conversation With Michka Assayas,* The Berkley Publishing Group, New York, New York, 2005, p.41

we do not come to the end of our days filled with wishes, regrets, and "should haves". We get *Where We Need To Go BY Discovering & Living Our* **LIFEFIT**.

However, this doesn't sound like many people in the world today. Very few are sure about why they were born: about their own personal **LIFEFIT.** Much has been made of the fact that today, as never before, people change their careers anywhere from 4-8 times throughout their lifetime. Students in university or college are staying in school far longer today, spending tens of thousands of dollars in the process, all trying to *"find themselves"*. We joke about *"professional students"*, knowing full well that people should not devote the majority of their lives to sitting in a classroom, but living their purpose for being. Surely it makes more sense to figure out *Where You Need To Go*, and then plot a path to get there. We need to discover clarity about *Where We Need To Go*, and the focus of this book is precisely that.

Figuring Out Where You Need To Go...

1. *Keeps You Secure* – One of the leaders of the early Christian church made a statement that speaks to the security of a person who has *Figured Out Where They Need To Go*. Paul the Apostle said in I Corinthians 15: *"...by the grace of God I am what I am..."*. This statement brings to mind the words of another great man, Popeye, when he said: *"I yam what I yam, and that's all that I yam...."*. To me, truly being secure is having a clear view of what and who you are, and who you are not. Insecure people are always trying to be someone they are *not*, or are trying to avoid being the person *they are*. *Figuring Out Where You Need To Go* prevents this.

2. *Keeps You From Comparison* – When you *Figure Out Where You Need To Go*, there is never any need to compare yourself to others. I remember, years ago, when I started out as a 20-year old public speaker and pastor, I was insecure in who and what and where I was. As a result, I lived a miserable, fear- and anxiety-filled life which almost drove me out of the profession. It

wasn't until I *Figured Out Where I Need To Go* that I even began to have a semblance of personal security and confidence. This came from *within*, not from *without*. Insecure people are always comparing, and comparison leads to one of two things: Inflation or Deflation. We either inflate and puff ourselves up in pride when we compare ourselves to others, or we deflate and tear ourselves down. Neither is a healthy way to live! When I am secure, *I won't dare to compare because I won't care. Figuring Out Where You Need To Go* helps you be secure in who YOU are.

3. *Keeps You Happy* – True happiness comes when you *Figure Out Where You Need To Go*. When you do, happiness and contentment become a real possibility. This world teaches us that happiness and contentment come as a result of the accumulation of wealth or possessions or prestige, but how can anyone be truly happy if they do not live for the reason they were born and "respect their wiring"? Each one of us is *wired* differently, with no two personalities, passions, pasts, or gift-mixes completely alike. 'Respecting your wiring' speaks of flowing with the way you were wired, and not trying to be something other than who and what you are. You ALREADY ARE something! All you need to do is find it and fulfill it: to *Figure Out Where You Need To Go*.

4. *Keeps You From Burnout* – Burnout can occur when we try to get somewhere we don't need to go. Burnout is caused in 2 situations…

When we are NOT Going Where *We* Need To…

When we ARE Going Where *We* Need To, But In A Way That Goes Against The Grain… The grain of who and what we are. Going against the grain causes a drain.

When we *Figure Out Where We Need To Go,* and are flowing with it, as opposed to getting drained of energy, we are fueled with energy!

5. *Keeps You On Track* – When you have no vision or clarity, you cast off restraint and personal discipline. It is easy to lose focus. The power of a vision is that it captures and captivates your heart, and harnesses your potential. It keeps you on track. Our

vision can be so clear that becomes a Life Road-Map, a map which gives us a personal and internal GPS. People who have a clear vision do not lose focus. They know where to run. *Figuring Out Where You Need To Go* provides you with this clear focus.

6. *Keeps You Winning* – Life is a battle. It is a daily war. As a matter of fact, it seems the more we go after *Where We Need To Go,* the harder it becomes. The path of least resistance provides precisely that: least resistance. When we give ourselves with reckless abandonment to *Figuring Out Where We Need To Go*, not only do we attract resistance, but everything becomes harder because the standards we set for ourselves inch higher. The good news is that not only does *Figuring Out Where You Need To Go attract* some resistance, it also gives us the energy to *power through* resistance. *Figuring Out Where You Need To Go* provides us with internal fuel which gets renewed daily!

7. *Keeps You From Unhealthy Choices* – Years ago my world-view was narrowly defined by a strict prism of either *"right"* or *"wrong"*, of either *"light"* or *"darkness"*. As time has gone on, I have come to realize that life is a lot more about what is *healthy* versus what is *unhealthy*. And I have also discovered that when I am going after *Where I Need To Go*, and am not side-tracked, I tend to make healthier choices for myself, my finances, my lifestyle and my family. A clear focus on *Where I Need To Go* helps me weed out what is unhealthy and superfluous. This can only be positive in the short and long term.

This bring us to the focus of this book on *Getting Where You Need To Go:*

21 Days. The significance of 21 Days cannot be overstated. 21 Days is what it takes to fully break bad habits, or to form new habits. Research has shown that it takes 21 Days to fully cultivate a new habit because 21 Days is the time required for new neuro-pathways to be fully formed in your brain.

Dr. Maxwell Maltz wrote the bestseller *"Psycho-Cybernetics"* in 1960. He was a plastic surgeon. He observed that it took 21 days for amputees to cease feeling phantom sensations in the amputated limb or to get used to their new face. And, further to that, he found it took 21 days to create a new habit. *"These, and many other common phenomena tend to show that it requires a minimum of about 21 days for an old mental image to dissolve and a new one to jell."*[3] Since that time, the "21-Day Habit Theory" has become an integral part of self-help programs.

"Brain circuits take engrams (memory traces), and produce neuro-connections and neuro-pathways only if they are bombarded for 21 days in a row. This means that our brain does not accept new data for a change of habit unless it is repeated each day for 21 days, without missing a day." [4]

Dr. Maltz noticed that many of his clients retained a poor self-image even after having surgery which improved their appearance. This prompted him to work with his clients' self-image prior to surgery. He discovered that he could partner with them to gain an improved self-image without surgery, using the same 21-day period to create changes in their mindset, and that surgery then became unnecessary in some cases.

Dr. Maltz carried this concept forward with a technique he called, *"Zero Resistance Living"*. The core of this method is simply to devote 15 minutes a day to the formation of any habit you wish to establish, and to do this regularly, consistently, and faithfully for 21 Days. By the 4th week, it should be easier to practice the new behavior than to slip back into the old patterns.

This book is all about change, metamorphosis, and personal growth. I would love to be part of permanent, transformative evolution in you! It is divided into the Introduction, and 13 Chapters, all with the purpose of helping us *Get Where We Need To Go*, and cultivating the habits that will lead to daily inspiration, personal growth and change. Seven of the chapters, from Chapter 4-10, are CORE CHAPTERS. These need to be read twice, one day after the other, to help the knowledge and information to seep in correctly and mark us: 21 Days.

---

[3] Dr. Maxwell Maltz. 1960. *Psycho-Cybernetics*. New York. Prentice-Hall, xiii.
[4] http://answers.google.com/answers/threadview/id/786165.html

This book presents a 21-Day Plan. Each chapter takes about 15 minutes to read. I encourage you to read this book in 21 Days, one chapter per day, and to read the CORE CHAPTERS twice, one day after the other. The concepts in these CORE CHAPTERS aren't complicated. But they do need focus, attention, and time to grasp in the context of *you* knowing *yourself*. Let the power of how your brain was wired work for you, to help you cultivate new habits, engineer new thoughts, and empower you to new ways of thinking and living.

As I said earlier, I have spent the last 15 years working with people. I love people, and have come to see that they ask about their own lives what any journalist asks about any good story: *Who? What? Where? When? Why? How? Who* am I? *What* am I supposed to be doing? *What* am I designed to do? *Where* should I aim to go? *Why* am I here? And, *How* and *When* will my destiny unfold? *When* and *How* will I get to the elusive *"There"?* These are fundamental life questions for anyone who desires to be truly happy and enjoy life!

This book will seek to answer these questions, and many more. I call this *Getting Where You Need To Go: Your* **LIFEFIT.** We will take an in-depth look at the concept of discovering and living our **LIFEFIT**; your unique combination of passions, interests, gifts, personality, talents, abilities, marketable skills, education, experiences, training, people skills, calling, networking, relationships, and oppor-tunities that is your personal *Sweet Spot*. This is your personal Winning Lottery Ticket, that place in your life where everything seems to fall into place. This is our **LIFEFIT:** our unique and distinctive shape. Join with me on this journey of self-discovery and living a life that counts, as we seek to *Get Where We Need To Go.*

The 21 Day Plan To Get You Going

Day 1 – Introduction – The 21-Day Plan To Get You Going!

Part 1 – You Have A "Why" And A "Where"

Day 2 – **Chapter 1** – You Have A *"Why"* , The Need For Purpose

Day 3 – **Chapter 2** – Living Without Regret

Day 4 – **Chapter 3** – You Have A *"Where"*: Your Personal Sweet
Spot & The Concept Of Your **"L.I.F.E.F.I.T."**

Day 5 – **Chapter 4 –** **L** – *Learning About* Your *Passions*

Day 6 – **Chapter 4 –** **L** – *Learning About* Your *Passions*

Day 7 – **Chapter 5 –** **I** – *Investigating* Your *Personality*

Day 8 – **Chapter 5 –** **I** – *Investigating* Your *Personality*

Day 9 – **Chapter 6 –** **F** – *Finding Out* Your *Gifts & Abilities*

Day 10 – Chapter 6 – **F** – *Finding Out* Your *Gifts & Abilities*

Day 11 – Chapter 7 – **E** – *Exploring* & Clarifying Your *Mission*

Day 12 – Chapter 7 – **E** – *Exploring* & Clarifying Your *Mission*

Day 13 – Chapter 8 – **F** – *Facilitating* & Developing
Marketable Skills

Day 14 – Chapter 8 – **F** – *Facilitating* & Developing
Marketable Skills

Day 15 – Chapter 9 – **I** – *Including Networking* & *Relationships*

Day 16 – Chapter 9 – **I** – *Including Networking* & *Relationships*

Day 17 – Chapter 10 – T – *Taking Opportunities* As They Arise

Day 18 – Chapter 10 – T – *Taking Opportunities* As They Arise

Part 2 – There Is A "How"

Day 19 – Chapter 11 – *Getting There:* The Power Of Your Choices

Day 20 – Chapter 12 – *Getting There:* Habits & Time Management

Day 21 – Chapter 13 – *Getting There:* Coaching & Mentoring

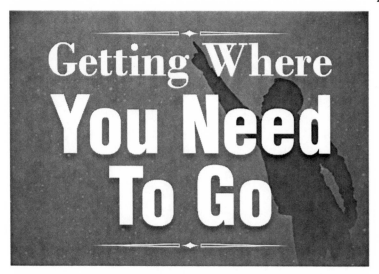

Part 1

You Have A *"Why"* And A *"Where"*

"Some people hear their own inner voices
with great clearness,
and they live by what they hear.
Such people become crazy,
or they become legends...

Legends of the Fall, 1994, Tristar Pictures

Getting Where You Need To Go
Chapter 1 – *You Have A **Why***
The Need For Purpose

When I was 6 years old, I had an experience that changed my life forever. Now, before someone interjects that a 6-year old cannot have life changing experiences, be reminded that all over the world, 6-year olds are having life changing experiences. Six year olds have life changing experiences, like everyone else – some positive and some negative; some nurturing and some harmful; some healing and some hurtful; some affirming and some abusive. The little girl with an abusive father; the small boy who has difficulty relating to others; the child who struggles in school; the weak one victimized by bullying; those raised in homes with economic disadvantages; all of these children have life-changing experiences at a very early age. What follows here is simply *my* personal experience. I have great respect for each person's own experiences.

My mother had recently moved her life in a spiritual direction. She had experienced the joy of spiritual surrender as she invited a Higher Power to come into her life and rescue her from a past of hurt, rejection and unmet needs. She used to watch a daily spiritual program on TV. As a 6-year old, I didn't watch it often, but one day found myself watching this TV program in Oshawa, Ontario, as the man spoke of spiritual surrender. He said that if anyone wanted to experience spiritual transformation and growth, they could call the number on the screen, and he would pray with them.

My own father had left when I was 2 years old, and I had experienced painful and abusive experiences with men for the next several years. I desperately needed a father; one who would care, nurture and affirm me for who I was. It seemed, as I listened to the man on the television, that spiritual surrender to this Higher Power would fill my need. I asked my mother if I could call the number. I phoned that day and began a personal spiritual relationship with God the Father as I understood Him.

24

Honestly, as a 6-year old boy, my experience was that my life began to change from that day forward. I began to experience an intimate spiritual relationship with God. I felt His love and affection for me, and He started to paint a picture on the canvas of my heart of His purpose and destiny for me. Until then I had no sense of purpose. I didn't believe there was a unique and special purpose for MY life. Suddenly I began to feel singular. I was one of a kind. I had been placed on the planet for a reason.

My life began to brim over with purpose, with destiny, with a cause. People who live without *"a reason"* often live very *unreasonable* lives! People who live without *"a point"* often miss *"the point"* of everything and everyone around them. When people have a sense of purpose, they believe in themselves, they can believe in others, and they can achieve unbelievable things. As the writings of an ancient Hebrew Proverb so eloquently say: *"Where there is no vision, the people perish."* When people lack this sense of a why, even getting out of bed can be a project involving government infrastructure grants and Antony Robbins' level motivation!

My life began to bubble over with a sense that I mattered, that I was unique and valuable; and because of that, I ended up at the complete opposite place that "they" said I should be. See, all of the people who study people like me, those of us abandoned by our father and deeply wounded in primary relationships, say I should have ended up in a far different place than I am today. The reality is only 34% of children will live with both biological parents through age 18 [5]. Boys without fathers are twice as likely to drop out of school, twice as likely to go to jail, and nearly 4 times as likely to need treatment for emotional and behavioural problems as boys with fathers.[6]

The National Center on Addiction & Substance Abuse at Columbia University found that children in 2-parent families with only a fair or poor relationship with their fathers were at 68%

[5] Dr. James Dobson. 2001. *Bringing Up Boys*. Wheaton, Illinois: Tyndale House Publishers, p.54.
[6] Ibid., 55

higher risk of smoking, drinking, and drug use than teens with a good or excellent relationship with their dads. [7]

Children who grow up with only one of their biological parents, compared to children who grow up with both parents, are 3 times more likely to become teen mothers, twice as likely to drop out of high school, and 1.4 times more likely to be out of school and work. [8]

Similar conclusions have been reached by many other scholars. Research conducted by the National Center for Health Statistics looked at a sample of 17,000 children aged 17 years and under. It found that, *"young people from single-parent families or step families were 2 or 3 times more likely to have had emotional and behaviour problems than those who had both of their biological parents present in the home."* [9]

One study of the effects of divorce was done in Sweden. It followed into their teenage years all children born in Stockholm in 1953 (and still living there in 1963) – some 7,719 males and 7,398 females. Focusing on psychiatric disturbances, they found *"the experience of family disruption involving parental separation or divorce has negative effects on later mental health wherever it occurs and regardless of the socioeconomic status of the household or of later changes in family structure"*. Boys born to unmarried women who got married and then later divorced had an especially high rate of psychological impairment by the age of 17. [10]

60% of America's rapists, 72% of adolescent murderers and 70% of long-term prison inmates come from fatherless homes [11]. University of Texas sociologists Ronald Angel and Jacqueline Angel conclude "father absence places children at a elevated risk of impaired social development, hinders their school performance, and, ultimately, can limit their chances for optimal social

---

[7] Ibid., 58.
[8] David Popenoe. 1996. *Life Without Father.*
New York: Simon and Schuster, p.4.
[9] Ibid., 56-57.
[10] Ibid., 58.
[11] Ibid., 63.

mobility… we can say with great confidence that father absence is… a mental health risk factor for the children."[12]

See, fatherlessness impacts negatively on almost all aspects of a child's life. The child is apt to have more emotional, behavioural, and physical health problems; he or she has more difficulties in school and drops out at a much higher rate. Girls are more likely to become unwed teen mothers. Problems often linger into adulthood, with the children of single-parent families facing a much higher risk of complications in their own marriages and parenting experiences. A sense of a lack of worth, lack of value and lack of purpose pervades to the core.

Those stats should have been me. But at the tender age of six, all of that changed when I found a sense of purpose and personal value. The infiltration of purpose changed everything. Discovering my personal purpose exposed my personal potential and filled my life with personal power. It helped me to believe in myself when others didn't, encouraged me when others wouldn't, and inspired me when others couldn't. Ralph Waldo Emerson said, *"There is no defeat except from within. There is really no insurmountable barrier save your own inherent weakness of purpose."* [13]

Deep in the heart of every person, there lies a profound desire to answer questions such as, *"Who Am I"?, "Why Am I Here"?, "What Was I Born To Do"?* We have to know our personal why. This purpose pulsates in the heart of every human being on this planet. We can suppress it, deny it, and misdirect it, but we can't kill it. Without living your purpose, life becomes an endless stream of activities and accomplishments, but is largely lived in emptiness and lack of fulfilment. Each and every one of us was born into this world with an incredible need for purpose, for meaning, for significance. Fyodor Dostoyevsky said that *"The secret of a man's being is not only to live but to have something to live for."*

---

[12] Ibid., 56.
[13] Derrick Sweet, 2002, *"Healthy Wealthy and Wise"*,
Toronto, Ontario: The Healthy Wealthy and Wise Corporation, p.5

Without a sense of purpose, life for humanity is nothing more than a victory in the life and death struggle of the survival of the fittest; the latest stage in a battle that started when we crawled out of the primordial soup and set out to prove we were stronger than the amoeba next to us. Without a purpose, we get into so much we would not get into if we had a purpose. It reminds me of Joanne...

I can still hear her cries piercing the night in the homeless shelter where I was privileged to do some part-time work. *"It hurts!... (sob)... It hurts so bad!... (cry)... Can't anyone do anything about this pain?... (sob)... It just hurts so bad! (cry)..."* She would quiet down for a moment, and then begin again. *"It hurts!... (sob)... It hurts so bad! (cry)... Can't anyone do anything about this pain? (sob)... It just hurts so bad!... (cry)...".* On and on she cried. She'd let go of all self-control. The pain was just too great. Her pain interrupted the sleep of the 30 women in the room with her, and 150 men on the other side of a barrier separating the men from the women. The homeless shelter was used to evening interruptions. But Joanne's pain was exceptional. Finally we called Emergency Medical Services.

To back up for a moment, when Joanne walked into the shelter, she appeared to be fine. She seemed cheerful and pleasant as always. She signed in, went straight to bed, and appeared to be in no pain at all. But, Joanne struggles with addiction, and our best guess is that as she fell asleep and her drugs wore off, the pain, which the drugs so skilfully masked, was now being exposed. The pain was always there, but was not felt because of the anaesthetic value of her drug.

If you knew Joanne, you would be shocked that she wrestles with addiction. She is bright, intelligent, beautiful, and dignified. She takes care of herself and those around her. But once, she opened up with me and shared her story. She gave glimpses into her lost sense of worth and purpose – the gaps in her life that were being plugged with drugs. Addiction took over as a way to dull the pain. A life without purpose can become so empty that we can frantically seek to fill the void in ways that can be harmful to ourselves and to others. So many feel either they have lost their purpose, or they never had one to begin with. They feel they are just a number, just one in a series of many of the same kind. Surely there is more purpose and reason to life than just that.

The greatest tragedy is not death, but life without a reason. It is dangerous to be alive and not know why you were given life. We need to think about our purpose. Purpose is:

The original reason for the existence of something,

The cause for the creation of an object,

The intent in the mind of the creator that motivated him to create something, The *why?*

Many feel no purpose. They are busy making a living but experience very little of life. Without knowing your purpose, life becomes an endless string of activities with little or no significance. A life without purpose is like a rocking horse... it moves a lot, and has lots of activity, but actually gets nowhere!

Those with no sense of purpose are like Alice in Alice in Wonderland. In a chat between Alice and the Cheshire Cat, Alice asked, *"Would you tell me please, which way I ought to go from here?" "That depends a good deal on where you want to get to,"* said the cat. *"I don't much care where,"* said Alice. *"Then it doesn't matter which way you go..."*, said the cat. Tragically, some act like it doesn't matter which way they go and what they do, because they are not yet gripped with a sense of purpose and destiny to *Get Where They Need To Go.*

Hope and purpose are as essential to life as air and water. We need hope to cope! Dr. Bernie Siegel found he could predict which cancer patients would go into remission by asking, *"Do you want to live to be 100?"* Those with a deep sense of purpose answered yes and were the ones most likely to survive! [14] When you lose your why, you can say, "Good-Bye"...

I've had an unmistakable knowing of my "Why" since I was 6 years old, but everyone is different. In this book, we'll look at the different places people seek to find their purpose, and begin

---

[14] Dr. Bernie Siegel, 1986, *Love, Medicine, And Miracles:* 1998: Harper Collins Publishing, Scarborough, Ontario

the process of plugging people into their purpose: their **LIFEFIT**. As I sit down to write this, I hope this offering will be one in which people can discover themselves, and yet also move past "self-discovery" into living a life that counts. So much of our culture and self-help industry today is geared towards the elusive goal of self-discovery, as if to say that self-discovery in itself leads to happiness, contentment, and fulfilment. The truth is that if self-discovery is the end goal, then self-discovery actually becomes very unsatisfying and unfulfilling, almost like the feeling one gets after getting stuffed with turkey on Thanksgiving. Self-discovery is crucial, but it ought to be one step on the journey toward living a life that counts.

Deep in the heart of every person is a profound desire to answer questions such as, *"Who Am I"?, "Why Am I Here"?, "What Was I Born To Do"?* There is a purpose that pulsates in the heart of every human being on this planet. We can suppress it, deny it, and misdirect it, but we can't kill it. When we think about *Getting Where We Need To Go*, we need to understand each of us was born for a specific reason. We were meant to go to a certain place. Purpose answers the question: "Why were you born?"

Let's examine in more detail why we need a purpose.

Purpose *Captivates* – Our heart, our attention, and our focus. Without a clear sense of our purpose, we will not reach our full potential. The laser beam of clear purpose inspires us to clear out the clutter, live a disciplined life, and *Get Where We Need To Go*. The tragedy of life is this: perhaps many people fail to reach their full potential because they spend too much time and effort chasing secondary, rather than primary, goals. As Andy Stanley said: *"If you really want to make a lasting impact, then you need to eliminate what you do well for the sake of what you can potentially do best."* [15] In 2009, the world was in shock as General Motors, once the pre-eminent king of the world-wide automotive industry, declared bankruptcy and only survived when the U.S. and

---

[15] Andy Stanley, *7 Practices Of Effective Ministry:* 2004: Multnomah Publishers, Sisters, Oregon, p.100

Canadian governments stepped in and provided life support. Perhaps their failure was caused by the relentless commitment to trying to *be* and to *do* everything: producing cars under 18 different brands and countless models, rather than focusing in on what brands did best and maximizing value in those categories. When you "get" your purpose, your purpose "gets" you, and does not let go. Purpose captivates your heart and mind to achieve your dream and *Get You Where You Need To Go.*

Purpose *Creates* – One seed of purpose inside you contains the power of Creation itself. Friedrich Wilhelm Nietzsche said: *"Everyone thinks that the principal thing to the tree is the fruit, but in point of fact the principal thing to it is the seed." [16]* All of us long for the fruit... but the seed is the key. The entire purpose of a seed is simply to germinate life, given the right conditions. Within one seed is enough life to plant a forest, grow a farm, and feed a community. Within the seed of our personal purpose is enough to create rich and lasting fruit for ourselves, our families and all those we care about.

Purpose *Calls* – Purpose has the ability to call us to something higher than ourselves. There is an awesome purpose for us as individuals: a rich, fulfilling, vibrant place *Where We Need To Go.* There is an incredible purpose for you, greater than simply you. Sadly, some have been conditioned to think and believe the lie, "It's all about me". It reminds me of the story of the little boy and his sister who were playing on a swing set one day. At first, they began by sharing the swing, but that didn't work so well. As they were jostling for position on the swing, the little boy looked at his sister. With all sincerity, he advised her, *"You know, if one of us would just get off the swing, there would be more room for me...".* This is some people's attitude throughout their entire lives: *"...there would be more room for me...".* Our purpose calls us to

---

[16] Mark Victor Hansen and Robert G. Allen, *The One Minute Millionaire:* 2002: Harmony Books, New York, New York, p.18

a higher way of living, not limited by selfishness and a "me-centric" mentality. George Bernard Shaw wrote: *"This is the true joy of life: being used up for a purpose recognized by yourself as a mighty one; being a force of nature instead of a feverish, selfish little clot of ailments and grievances, complaining that the world will not devote itself to making you happy."* Your purpose calls you to *Get Where You Need To Go!*

Purpose *Clarifies* – Some are confused about *Where They Need To Go*. They don't really know *Where They Need To Go* primarily because they lack a clear sense of purpose. I once heard that the seven ages of man are as follows: *"spills, drills, thrills, bills, ills, pills, and wills"*. Some live life like that, just going from one stage, one place, to the next. They never stop to ask what their specific purpose as an individual is. Purpose is a wonderful thing because it becomes an internal GPS, a built-in guidance system that clarifies a path for you to follow. With so many options available to us in the global economy, we can waste huge segments of our lives simply seeking to find ourselves. We need to minimize the *"lost decades"*, so to speak. Being gripped by your purpose does just that, and tells you *Where You Need To Go*.

Purpose *Connects* – An amazing thing happens to us on the way to fulfilling our purpose and *Getting Where We Need To Go*: we find others who are headed in the same direction. Having worked in a homeless shelter for the last 10 plus years, I have found, time and time again, the remarkably deep and true bond that comes between staff and volunteers and care-givers in a place like that. Because generally we are all focused around the values of caring for the needs of the homeless, believing that people matter, and having a base point of compassion and understanding, there is an incredibly profound connection between us. This same dynamic plays out in cause after cause and purpose after purpose, be it environmental protection or human rights issues or mentoring entrepreneurs or in our political affiliations – in fact, in everything we do. Purpose connects us to the world around us and draws us away from loneliness and isolation. The only thing more satisfying than *Getting Where You Need To Go,* is *Getting Where You Need To Go* with partners, team members, and supporters.

Purpose *Completes* – People who are in hot pursuit of their purpose; who are *Getting Where They Need To Go*, are generally happier and more complete than those who are simply drifting along. As Charles Allen said, *"Miserable are the persons who do not have something beyond themselves to search for."* [17] People who do not fulfill their purpose in life, and who do not *Get Where They Need To Go*, generally live with regret. An intriguing sociological study [18] asked 50 people over the age of 95 one question: *'If you could live your life over again, what would you do differently?'* Three answers continually emerged and dominated the results of the study:

- If I had to do it over again, I would reflect more.
- If I had to do it over again, I would risk more.
- If I had to do it over again, I would do more things that would live on after I'm dead.

This shows us that many come to the end of their lives and have regrets. When we live our lives with purpose and *Get Where We Need To Go*, we live a more complete life, and generally live without regret. And that is the focus of our next chapter...

---

[17] Glenn Van Ekeren, *Speaker's Sourcebook II:* 1994: Prentice Hall, Paramus, New Jersey, p.307
[18] James Emery White, *You Can Experience A Purposeful Life:* 2000: Word Publishing, Nashville, Tenn.

Getting Where You Need To Go
Chapter 2 –
Living Without Regret

When 50 people, aged 95 and over, are asked what they might do differently, and consistent answers come to the surface[19], this shows us that many come to the end of their lives and experience *regret*. When we live our purpose and *Get Where We Need To Go*, we live a full and abundant life, and generally live life without regret. People who don't fulfill their purpose in life, and who don't *Get Where They Need To Go*, generally come to the end, and have regret. Here we want to discuss *Living Without Regret*.

Several years ago I was reading the newspaper, when my attention was gripped by a headline. The caption in the National Post, on January 11, 2001, read, " 'I owe my life' to priest who prevented abortion, Dion tells magazine." As I read the article, I discovered that it referred to the world-famous singer, Celine Dion, who said that she owed her life to a local parish priest who convinced her mother _not_ to abort her. The singer said her mother was devastated when she found she was pregnant with Celine, her 14th child. So, her mother went to the local priest for advice. She was considering ending her pregnancy. The priest pleaded with her to keep God's gift, as revealed in this child. As a result of this conversation, Celine's mother chose not to abort her. As I am sure you can imagine, Celine feels she owes her life to this priest.

Think about this with me. Celine Dion, probably Canada's best known musical artist ever, and one of the most successful artists in the world, was almost never born. She has recorded over 200 songs in 5 different languages, and sold over 150 million albums world-wide. She has won Junos, Grammies, World Music Awards, and every other musical award one could win. Yet, before her destiny ever had a chance to come to pass, it was almost never revealed. Before she ever saw the light of day, her life almost did not blossom. All that potential and talent would never have been

---

[19] James Emery White, *You Can Experience A Purposeful Life:* 2000: Word Publishing, Nashville, Tenn.

realized. This is not about how we may feel about the right to life or the right to choose, but about the possibility of potential not fully realized.

All of us would agree that for Celine Dion to have never lived, to have never breathed and created artistically and grown, would have been a tragedy of unimaginable proportions. To never have seen the light of day and not draw us into her exceptionally talented music would have left this world a darker place. Celine has a destiny, a purpose, a reason for being, a **LIFEFIT**, which is clearly to create, write and perform music. To have never lived this **LIFEFIT** would have hurt us all.

But what about you? You may not be Celine, but will you grasp and embrace your personal destiny? Seeing that you are designed with a purpose, with a specific **LIFEFIT**, are you ready to embrace your potential and brighten this world? Can you *see your destiny* so you can *seize the day*? Clearly, there is somewhere you need to go. When you see your destiny, you will be empowered to seize your days! *All* of them! If we do not fulfill that destiny, others may miss out, like we all might have without Celine. How might your world suffer, your business suffer, your friends suffer, your family suffer, if you do not *Get Where You Need To Go?*

Sometimes we find purpose in the strangest places, like I did one day with Joe H. To this day, a few years later, I still don't understand why Joe chose me. Joe is a client at the largest homeless shelter in Canada, where I served part-time as an Adult Care Worker. Joe had been on a bit of a bender that night, which wasn't unusual. What was unusual was how he got there. I looked over at him as he lay on the floor. We had run out of sleeping mats. There he was with a tube of hair gel in his mouth. He was seeking some "medication" to help him through his pain. From a policy standpoint, I needed to confiscate his chosen inebriant. He soon passed out. Having seen hairspray, mouthwash, glue, and even Lysol used as a method of intoxication, it was not unusual to see this. People will go to incredible lengths to cope with the pain within.

A few hours later, Joe H. woke up and seemed to have

sobered up. At that point, he made quiet motions to me to come over to him. Not knowing what he needed, I went over. He began to break. Weeping and crying, he told me how sad he was with his life, about all of his regrets, and how disappointed he was with where he had ended up. He labours under the pain of a serious injury that hinders his ability to be and do what he loves: hard work. As so many of us would when faced with life-debilitating circumstances, he turned to alcohol and drugs to try to medicate the pain of what he perceived to be his useless life. In his broken sobs, he communicated to me that he was suicidal and that he was right on the edge of ending it all.

I continued to let him pour out his heart and share details of his pain. He told me how he felt boxed in with no other choice in coping with the pain except for ending his life. As he continued to pour out his feelings and emotions, I knew he needed to let it all out before he would come anywhere close to being mentally or emotionally ready to hear anything I had to say.

About 45 minutes later, I knew my opportunity was there. I can't remember exactly what I said, and I can't remember what he said back, but all I know is, when we were done, Joe H. had decided he would live for another day. I do remember communicating to him his incredible worth and value, that he is uniquely precious and indispensable to his family who know and love him. We discussed his significance and importance as a human being at great length. But on that day, Joe H. might have ended it all because of the pain of regret and the pain of living without a sense of worth, value and purpose.

See, we all have a purpose! We don't have to live with regret. We each have a **LIFEFIT** that is specific to us. We're happy and content when we flow with our **LIFEFIT**. It is far easier to work *with* the grain of our **LIFEFIT** than *against* it. Each of us was designed to do certain things. We are unique, wonderfully complex, a composite of many different factors. What we are made *to be* determines what we are intended *to do*. When your **LIFEFIT** doesn't match the role you play in life, you feel like a square peg being forced into a round hole, frustrating yourself and others. Not only does it produce limited results, it is also a waste of your gifts, your time, and energy. When we are living our

LIFEFIT, we experience peace in our hearts and rest in our minds. Even at work, when we flow with our **LIFEFIT,** we replenish and refuel. Imagine that!

People desperately need a sense of purpose, a sense of destiny. It is crucial. Purpose Is:

The Original Reason For The Existence Of Something,
The Intent In The Mind Of The Creator To Create Something,
The "Why?
Where You Need To Go...

~ Each Of Us Was Born For A Specific Reason ~
PURPOSE ANSWERS THE QUESTION:
"WHY WERE YOU BORN?"
~ WE MUST FIND THE ANSWER TO THIS QUESTION
AND LIVE THE ANSWER TO BE HAPPY ~

The greatest tragedy is not death, but life without a cause. It is risky to be alive and not know why you were given life. Many have no purpose… they are busy making a living but experience very little of life. Without knowing your purpose and **LIFEFIT**, life becomes an endless string of activities with little or no significance. A life lived outside of its **LIFEFIT** is like a rocking horse or a carousel: it moves a lot but gets nowhere.

Purpose *Feeds* Us – A clear sense of purpose feeds and fulfills us. William Cowper, an English poet who lived in the 1700s, went so far as to say, *"The only true happiness comes from squandering ourselves for a purpose."* We are all *"squandering"* our lives on something. Are you *"squandering"* yours on your purpose? For each of us, that purpose is different, but for us all, that specific purpose brings us happiness and joy.

Purpose *Leads* Us – Clarity is key in this information age. With so much information coming at us, it is crucial that we have a clear sense of what to do and where to go. Purpose provides this internal direction and leading. Once again, the words of the Buddha provide guidance here: *"Your work is to discover your work, and then with all your heart, to give yourself to it."*

Purpose *Weeds* Us – One of the keys to clarity is the ability to say no: no to distractions, deviations and directions not connected to your purpose. Many say yes to everything because they feel guilt or obligation or responsibility... to things not really connected to their purpose. *Getting Where You Need To Go* is liberating because it gives freedom to say no.

Purpose *Seeds* Us – Each and every day, as a result of having a clear sense of personal purpose, **LIFEFIT** people are inspired and infused with innovation and ideas. Not a day goes by when ideas and concepts and thoughts and solutions and plans and inspiration do not have the opportunity to fill their hearts and minds. There is an internal, overflowing abundance coming from their sense of personal purpose. This is not to say that tough days don't come, but knowing your purpose will seed you and inspire you time and time again. The creative juices flow better in us and through us when we live better connected to our personal purpose.

As you may have discovered, my personal philosophy of life and world-view includes the thought that each and every one of us was specifically designed by a Caring and Careful Designer, who purposefully crafted our very selves in the specific way He wanted us. Sacred writings declare, *"...we are God's masterpiece. He has created us... so that we can do the good things He planned for us long ago."* [20] I passionately declare that this is true, and in this book I call this precise blueprint our **LIFEFIT**; which is our unique and person-specific design.

---

[20]*Holy Bible*, New Living Translation, copyright 1996 by Tyndale Charitable Trust, Ephesians 2:10

Discovered Or Determined?

Each of us has an exclusive **LIFEFIT**. In essence, this is the way that we were wired; how we were programmed. To be truly happy and successful in this life, we need to clarify and comprehend, and then live out our **LIFEFIT**. This **LIFEFIT** is not something we determine for ourselves, but it is something that we discover about ourselves. You and I can no more determine our personal **LIFEFIT** than a giraffe can choose to be a giraffe, or an elephant can choose to be an elephant. But, we do choose whether to live and actualize our **LIFEFIT** or not. Will we be who we are meant to be and fulfill our potential?

Remember: it is crucial to discover this *"Why?"*, because when you lose your *"Why?"*, you can say *"Good-Bye"*. Without a sense of purpose, people can easily become discouraged, can rapidly fall into depression, and can effortlessly fall into despair. We are devastated when we lack that sense of destiny that defines who and what we are.

So the question here is, "How do you discover the purpose you were created for?" How do you understand *Where You Need To Go*? How can you *discover* and then *live* your personal **LIFEFIT**? We have two options:

Speculate... What most people do. They surmise, postulate, and theorize. They spend years and years taking "General Studies" programs in university, years and years reading self-help books and self-actualization books and self-realization books and self-awareness books. Eventually, they either build the confidence to guess at something and try that, or they settle for comfortable living as a substitute. There's got to be a better way than speculation and guesswork when it comes to our future.

Validate... Validate *Where You Need To Go* based on your **LIFEFIT**. Design determines destiny... form reveals function. The best news you can hear all day is that there's an alternative to speculation and guesswork when it comes to your personal purpose! Your **LIFEFIT** leads you to discover *Where You Need To Go*. My WHO determines my WHAT and my WHERE. When you look at nature, for example, a bird, you can see the meticulous and precise nature of its design. Everything about a bird, from its aerodynamic beak, to its feathers and their flight ability, to its light body, has been physiologically designed with one single purpose: to fly. When you look at a fish, from its scales to its fins to its system of breathing, you can see it was designed to swim. It's the same with you. Everything about you has been perfectly designed to flow with your **LIFEFIT**. The single riveting purpose for your life is for you to know and flow with your specific **LIFEFIT**.

This world teaches us that happiness and contentment come as a result of the accumulation of wealth, possessions, or prestige. But how can anyone be truly happy if they do not live for the reason they were born; if they do not respect their wiring? All of us were wired differently, with no two personalities, passions, pasts, or mixtures of gifts completely alike! "Respecting your wiring" speaks of flowing with the way you were wired, and not trying to be someone or something you are not. You *already* are something and someone magnificent, so don't continue trying to become that. Acknowledge your awesome-ness. Bask in your brilliance! All you need to do now is find your magnificence and purpose and destiny and fulfill it. When we do that, we are at peace, replenished and content.

For each and every one of us, there is a genetic map which determines our make-up. This is like a recipe which determines the flavour, contours and essence of our lives. The first analysis of the entire set of human genetic instructions was published on February 11, 2001, the result of a 10-year, multi-billion-dollar international race to map the human genome. The results revealed that humans have far fewer genes than expected. Researchers also found genes are strikingly similar across all ethnic groups, with every person sharing 99.999% of their genetic code with the rest of the population.

"All the glorious differences among individuals in our species that can be attributed to genes falls in a mere 0.0001% of the [gene] sequence", says Dr. Craig Venter, president of Celera Genomics, in a long-awaited paper published in the journal Science, Feb.2001 Issue, Volume 291, No.5507.

All that distinguishes an Inuit from a Czech or an African, or Britney Spears from Diana Ross from you or I, are variations in 300,000 letters in a 3-billion-letter sequence in the human genome.

Scientists say while it might be easy to tell at a glance whether a person is Asian, African or Caucasian, the differences dissolve when one looks beyond surface features and scans the human genome for DNA hallmarks of race. Genetically, there are no races.

When I read that, something goes off inside. Though we are all 99.999% the same, we are 0.0001% different. There is a 3-billion letter genetic sequence that defines the essence of who we are. This 3-billion letter genetic code determines and forms our make-up. Now, for all humans, this 3-billion letter code is exactly the same, with the exception of 300,000 letters: 0.0001%. You and I, the black person and the white person, the Australian and the South American, the Caucasian and the Chinese, the Japanese and the Jew, are all exactly the same with the exception of that 0.0001% of our make-up which determines whether we become a Billy Graham or a Britney Spears, white or black, have blond hair or dark hair, are tall or short, have freckles or do not, have blue eyes or brown eyes, are bent toward mathematics or mechanics, medicine or ministry. It is that 0.0001% that this book is about.

See, with the genetic code of this 0.0001%, the essence of our make-up has been written right into the core of our being. Even though we are all 99.999% the same, we are 0.0001% different. This is our **LIFEFIT**. Grasping your personal purpose and living your **LIFEFIT** is key to living without regret.

5 Keys To Living Without Regret... DAILY "R.E.S.E.T."

I am a big believer in the role of daily routines, habit patterns, and practices in order to achieve daily results and long-term success. We may achieve success for a time without them, but long-term success is often about consistently applying ourselves to daily routines, habit patterns, and practices. Here are five daily practices which are keys to living without regret, built around the word **"R.E.S.E.T."**. Applying these keys daily helps us to live without regret.

<u>R</u> – **Re-Align With Your Personal Purpose** – Each day when I awake, I take time to contemplate and meditate upon my personal purpose. There was a time in my life when I would just wake up, go through my daily exercise routine and spiritual meditation, and then run off to face the day. But now, I intentionally take time to re-align myself with my personal purpose. I review my personal mission and visualize how I will seek to fulfil it in the day ahead, and avoid distraction. In my view, I see focusing on my personal purpose in the same way one could see an extremely sharp knife. No matter how sharp the blade may be, usage has a way of rendering it dull. The more it is used, the more we need to sharpen it. In the same way, life dulls our personal purpose. Life has so many ways of distracting us from our personal purpose and getting us focused purely on the daily grind. So, daily, we need to sharpen our focus and re-align with our personal purpose. This is my daily re-calibration of my internal GPS.

<u>E</u> – **Engage Your Power To Choose Your Personal Purpose** – After I have spent time re-aligning with my personal purpose, I engage my power of choice. I cannot control far more things in life than the things that I can control, but I can always guide my choices around working towards my personal purpose. So in the midst of the other pressures, responsibilities, and distractions, I choose again to focus on what matters, what's important, what will last beyond my lifetime: my personal purpose. Pursuing your personal purpose is all about making

choices and trade-offs; it's about deliberately choosing your personal purpose over other pursuits. So daily I seek to make the choice for my personal purpose.

S – Seek Supportive, Affirming Relationships – I was in a group coaching session just the other day, and one of the participants in that session asked a question I have heard several times before. The question went something like this: What if you are in a relationship with someone who is not supporting you as you pursue your personal purpose? It was clear that she was not describing a marriage relationship, but an important relationship to her nonetheless. The pain in her eyes told me the relationship had value and significance, but so also did her personal purpose. The answer I gave her, as a Life Coach, was that though I could not speak to her specific situation, in general, it is healthy to seek out relationships that support and affirm us as we pursue our personal purpose. My experience has been that when we are in a key relationship which does not support our personal purpose, in time, we begin to resent the relationship and the person, who we view as somehow holding us back. People who are serious about their personal purpose need to view meaningful relationships through the prism of their personal purpose, and be cautious in making choices regarding relationships.

E – Expect The Best, All The Time – There can be no doubt about the impact of our expectations and beliefs. When we chase after life hoping for the best, believing in the best, and expecting the best, generally, we have a better chance of getting there than when we do not! As Napoleon Hill said, *"What the mind can conceive, it can achieve"*. I hope we never end up in the misery, faithlessness, and hopelessness described in this Alexander Pope quote: *"'Blessed is the man who expects nothing, for he shall never be disappointed' was the ninth beatitude"*. That's a bleak place to be. We have all been in places where we have not felt like it, but we need to expect the best, all the time. You can't get to a place that you don't believe exists. For all of us, there are times when we feel we are just spinning our wheels; that we will never get where we need to go. So each day I take time to review my personal purpose, and to re-engage my sense of belief in myself and where I am going. After all, the only limits in your life are those that you set yourself. I take time to believe in myself, in my gifts and abilities, and in my personal purpose. I take time to believe again that I can get there, that I can do it, and that it's all worth it.

T – Take Time Each Day For Actions Connected To Your Personal Purpose – Take a moment with me and think about your future. Where will you be one month from today? Three months? Six months? Think of 1 year from today, 2 years, 3 years, or even 5. Where will you be, and more importantly, what will you be doing? The truth is that you will be exactly where you are today, 5 years from now, with the exception of the actions you live out today that will shape your future tomorrow. I will never get closer to my personal purpose tomorrow if I do not carve out time today, however small, to get there. Each day I carve out time to engage in activity that is connected to my personal purpose. I take the picture and I make it practical; the vision becomes reality; the dreaming becomes doing. If my goal is to finish another book, I carve out 60 minutes a day to write. If I want to achieve an athletic goal, I slice out 45 minutes for that. If it is to finish a certain project, I take time daily to engage actions which will inch me closer. A little time spent, each day, will get you much further than cramming large chunks sporadically. As Mark Twain said, *"The secret of getting ahead is getting started"*.

Confucius said: *"Choose a job you love, and you will never have to work a day in your life"*. As Stephen Covey puts it in his book, "The 8th Habit", we need to find our own voice, and then help others to find theirs. This sounds like a meaningful contribution to humanity; a life lived without regret. Each day, as we take time to do a **Daily R.E.S.E.T.**, we will move closer to our personal purpose. And, we will move closer to a life lived without regret; a life where we *Get Where We Need To Go*. True success is *Getting Where You Need To Go*. *Getting Where You Need To Go* is all about your personal "life mission": your **LIFEFIT:**

L – Learning About Your **Passions**

I – Investigating Your **Personality**

F – Finding Out Your **Gifts** & **Abilities**

E – Exploring & Clarifying Your **Mission**

F – Facilitating & Developing **Marketable Skills**

I – Including **Networking** & **Relationships**

T– Taking **Opportunities** As They Arise

Going forward, we will explore these elements of our **LIFEFIT** in depth. As we do, I hope all of us will avoid the fate of those who have in their obituary the scariest words ever said: *"Should Have Been"*. As an Ordained Minister, Counsellor, and Certified Life & Executive Master Coach, I have had the immense privilege of presiding over funerals packed with people who lived their **LIFEFIT;** who turned potential into reality and possibility into actuality. These rich and fulfilling lives impacted and bubbled over into the lives of many around them. They fulfilled their **LIFEFIT** and enriched others!

I have also done funerals with 1 or 2 people paying their respects at the graves of those who *should have been*. Empty funerals speaking of empty lives, devoid of knowing and flowing with their **LIFEFIT**. May we never have it said of us, *"should have been"*, *"could have been"*, or *"might have been"*. May the only thing in my obituary and yours say, ***"was"***… been there… done that. Life has so many ways of distracting us from our personal purpose. This book will help you find that by partnering with your to discover your **LIFEFIT**.

Getting Where You Need To Go
Chapter 3 – *You Have A "Where": Your Personal Sweet Spot & The Concept Of Your LIFEFIT*

In this chapter, I want to look at some principles that have really helped in the areas of personal growth, personal discovery, and achieving positive personal change within my own life. These will help you discover who you are, as well as to develop positive life strategies for *Getting From Where You Are* to *Getting Where You Need To Go:* your **LIFEFIT**. We can all use help moving from one *level* to the next.

In truth, there is a *breathtaking* place you need to go. Not a single one of us has yet "been there", or arrived at our ultimate destination. Just as none of us has experienced all that life has to offer, so none has yet completely arrived at where we as individuals need to go. So, we need to get *From Where We Are* to *Where We Need To Go!*

And, *Where You Need To Go* is different from *Where Others Need To Go.* We all have *Somewhere We Need To Go.* It's different from *Where Others Need To Go.* But we follow the same process to get there.

The first question we need to ask in *Getting Where We Need To Go* is *Where Am I Going?* What is my specific destiny as an individual? I once heard it said that the seven ages of man are: *"spills, drills, thrills, bills, ills, pills, wills".* Some people live their lives like that, just going from one stage, one place, to the next. They never stop to ask what is their specific destiny as an individual. I call this your **LIFEFIT.**

Let's Cultivate A Sense Of Destiny...

"When you discover your mission, you'll feel its demand. It will fill you with enthusiasm and a burning desire to get to work."
W. Clement Stone [21]

---

[21] http://www.brainyquote.com/quotes/authors/w/w_clement_stone_2.html

"Nothing is as necessary for success as the single-minded pursuit of an objective." [22] Frederick W. Smith

The greatest tragedy is not death, but life without a reason. It is dangerous to be alive and not know why you were given life. The reality is that the person who simply drifts into success in any area of human activity is almost as rare as the ship that drifts aimlessly into a safe harbour. Steven Covey, author of *"The Seven Habits of Highly Successful People"* teaches that one of these habits is to, *"Begin with the end in mind."*

I have often heard it said that more people fail through lack of purpose than lack of talent. All around us, we definitely do *not* have a talent deficit, but perhaps a deficit of purpose and even reason for being. This is why I am quick to say that *when you lose your why, you can say good-bye*. Those without a sense of destiny are like Alice in "Alice in Wonderland". In a chat with the Cheshire Cat, Alice asked, *"Would you tell me please, which way I ought to go from here?" "That depends a good deal on where you want to get to,"* said the cat. *"I don't much care where,"* said Alice. *"Then it doesn't matter which way you go..."*, said the cat.

I call *Where You Need To Go* your **LIFEFIT**: Your unique combination of passions, interests, gifts, personality, talents, abilities, marketable skills, education, experiences, training, people skills, calling, networking, relationships, and opportunities where you are blessed. We will not experience abundance doing anything, at any time, with anyone, anywhere, any how! We are empowered and blessed doing our **LIFEFIT** Thing, in our own **LIFEFIT** Time, with **LIFEFIT** Partners, in a way that flows in alignment with our **LIFEFIT**. This is your personal Winning Lottery Ticket, that place in your life where everything seems to fall into place. Our **LIFEFIT** is our unique and distinct shape. This is your personal place of harmony, abundance, potential, and manifestation, that place in your life where you attract all you need and long for.

---

[22] http://www.allmotivationalquotes.com/quote/frederick-w-smith-1/

No Fit Produces...

No Form – Life has shape, texture, and form when we know and flow with our **LIFEFIT**.

No Faith – Faith in ourselves and our potential (and that of others) comes as we know and flow with our **LIFEFIT**.

No Fun – Fully contented and happy people know and flow with their **LIFEFIT**.

No Faithfulness – We become rooted and anchored as we know and flow with our **LIFEFIT**.

No Favour – It seems like the sun shines on us when we know and flow with our **LIFEFIT**.

No Fragrance – Our lives are a sweet aroma when we know and flow with our **LIFEFIT**.

Each and every one of us is a work of art. Before we were born, we were each assigned a unique **LIFEFIT**. Like no two trees are alike, no two flowers, no two butterflies, even so, we are all unique. We all have a distinctive and exclusive **LIFEFIT** specific to us. We are happy and content when we flow with our **LIFEFIT**. It's far easier to work with the "grain" of our **LIFEFIT** than against it. Each of us was uniquely designed to do certain things. We are unique, wonderfully complex, a composite of many different factors. What you were made to *be* determines what you were intended to *do*. When your **LIFEFIT** doesn't match the role you play in life, you feel like a square peg in a round hole, frustrating yourself and others. Not only does it produce limited results, it is also a waste of your talents, time and energy. *To Get Where We Need To Go We Need To See Our* **LIFEFIT**:

48

L – Learning About Your **Passions**

I – Investigating Your **Personality**

F – Finding Out Your **Gifts & Abilities**

E – Exploring & Clarifying Your **Mission**

F – Facilitating & Developing **Marketable Skills**

I – Including **Networking & Relationships**

T – Taking **Opportunities** As They Arise

For all of us, at some point, the moment of truth arrives. Maybe in reading a book like this, or in listening to an inspiring speaker, or perhaps on a personal retreat to the mountains. The moment comes when we discover and uncover *why* we were born, and *who* and *what* we were born to *be* and *do!* Our eyes are opened to see our **LIFEFIT** to BE *someone* and to DO *something!*

Sometimes, we respond in fear, petrified to embrace who & what we are. We react to this moment of revelation, with fear and apprehension. It is easier to be a teacher than a *"life-shaper"*; safer to be a doctor than an *"improver of lives"*; less risky to be a lawyer than a *"defender of the weak"*. So, we run towards a career when we should be running towards our personal destiny: our **LIFEFIT**. Our career was only ever to be a vehicle to facilitate the fulfillment of our **LIFEFIT**. But some use it as an escape, so they can remain in mediocrity and anonymity.

See, this world teaches us that happiness and contentment come as a result of gathering wealth, possessions, position, or prestige. But, how can anyone be truly happy if they do not respect their wiring, and live out the reason they were born? Everyone of is was wired differently, with no two personalities, passions, pasts, or gift-mixes completely alike! Respecting your wiring speaks of flowing with the way you were wired, and not trying to be something you are not! You *already* are something; all you need to do is find it and fulfill your destiny!

Your Wiring Consists of...

- **Your Wishes** – Your *wiring* reflects your *wishes*, which, in essence, are your dreams. When you are *wired* a certain way, you begin to *wish* a certain way: to dream, imagine and visualize yourself achieving those things and leaving a positive footprint in alignment with those wishes.

- **Your Ways** – Your *wiring* reflects your *ways*: your subconsciously chosen methods of operation and the specific steps you instinctively take to solve problems, think creatively, deal with variables, and achieve results. We are all born with a certain *"way"* of learning, processing information, making decisions, and taking action. Our intuitive way of approaching life and situations is a part of our *wiring*.

- **Your Work** – Our *wiring* has an impact on the type of *work* we engage in and enjoy, and the kind of *work* we are good at. Simply put, our ability to be successful in our *work* involves us playing to strengths, and our strengths are shaped by how we are *wired*. Peter Drucker, the management guru, said something like this when he said, *"Efficiency, which is doing things right, is irrelevant until you work on the right things."*

- **Your Whys** – Understanding your *wiring* is one of the crucial keys to understanding what makes you tick. Self-awareness and self-discovery comes easily as we gain a clear grasp of the way we are *wired*. Your *"whys"* for the choices you make, the relationships you find yourself in, the career paths you go after, and the philosophies you embrace has a lot to do with your *wiring*. Your sense of personal mission, life purpose, and intrinsic calling (your *whys*) have a lot to do with how you were *wired* in the first place.

- **Your What** – Your *"what"*, which is your life tool-kit: your unique combination of gifts, talents, proficiencies and abilities, stems from your *wiring*. We are not simply the lucky winners of the survival of the fittest. We are unique works of art with specific skill sets, gift mixes and talent combinations that flow from how we are *wired*.

- **Your Well** – In ancient times, a *well* was considered to be a source of life. In dry, arid cultures, before the times of taps and water fountains, being without a *well* to from which draw water, and thus life, was a scary proposition. In a similar vein, many go through their lives not properly connected with their own unique *wiring* and thus unplugged from their personal *well:* their personal source of strength and sustenance. When I am flowing with my *wiring* and aligned with my **LIFEFIT**, I am continually refueled, replenished and renewed. When I go against the grain of my own *wiring*, it is draining and saps my energy. If you lack energy, it might be due to a lack of sleep or lack of exercise or an unhealthy diet, but it could also be because you are engaging in tasks that you are not properly *wired* to do. Consider that.

- **Your Wonder** – Each of us has a personal sweet spot; a place where what we do is unique and inspired and amazing. We all inhabit a space where we bring wonder and a sense of awe to others, because we are flowing with our *wiring* and excel at a particular skill or practice. I have often gasped in wonder when I have seen some of my coaches and mentors do what they are intuitively good at and flow with; be it writing or speaking or singing or creating or relating or building or caring or whatever. When we respect our *wiring*, it flow easily and naturally, and we bring a sense of *wonder* and awe to those around us.

A Tip About Getting Where You Need To Go...

For the rest of our journey together, we will discuss *Getting Where You Need To Go* in detail. *To Get Where We Need To Go We Need To See Our* **LIFEFIT**:

L – Learning About Your **Passions**

I – Investigating Your **Personality**

F – Finding Out Your **Gifts & Abilities**

E – Exploring & Clarifying Your **Mission**

F – Facilitating & Developing **Marketable Skills**

I – Including **Networking & Relationships**

T– Taking **Opportunities** As They Arise

We will break down each area and examine how we can discover these in our own lives and make room for them, and weave each component of our **LIFEFIT** into our actions. Before we do, I want to add a tip about *Getting Where You Need To Go...*

In Order To Get Where You Need To Go,
Being Willing To Move Forward From
Where You Currently Are Is Crucial.
Sometimes, we gotta give up to go up!

John Pierpont Morgan, who arranged the merger of Edison General Electric and Thompson-Houston Electric Company in 1892 to form General Electric, said: *"The first step towards getting somewhere is to decide that you are not going to stay where you are."* The first step towards getting somewhere is to decide that you are not going to stay where you are right now.

The opening scene in the hit animated movie Ice Age 2 is pretty amazing. It shows talking animals, in an Ice Age, rushing down waterslides and complaining about the heat. All the ice is melting and for the first time, many of these animals get to swim in the water, as opposed to navigating the ice.

The problem with the end of the Ice Age is the melting ice. At first it was a lot of fun for the animals, but the story of the movie is how all the animals have to leave their habitats and homes and move to a place where they won't be exposed to flooding and drown. They need to make it to the end of the valley, where there's a boat and safety. After all, as the animals say in the movie, *"The world's coming to an end! Fast Tony says the world's gonna flood"*. The animals are selling breathing devices and floatation devices to each other, and debating when all the ice will turn to water.

One of the scenes tells a story we see time and time again all around us. The porcupines are trying to pull Grandpa porcupine out of his hole so they can travel together to safety. Grandpa porcupine is refusing, saying, *"Well I'm not leaving... I was born in this hole, and I'll die in this hole."*

"I was born in this hole, and I'll die in this hole." We were all born in a hole of one kind or another, and frankly, we will all die in another hole. The question is, will they be the same holes? To *Get Where You Need To Go* you must be rock-solid determined to NOT die in the hole you were born in.

To *Get Where We Need To Go* we simply need to make a commitment to think new thoughts, believe new beliefs, and try new things. We need to choose to step away from our safe place, and go hard after our dreams, our goals, and living in a way that flows with how we are wired. We need to commit to living our **LIFEFIT**. Let's journey now together.

Getting Where You Need To Go
Chapter 4 – "L" –
Learning About Your Passions

Viktor Frankl said: *"Everyone has his own specific vocation or mission in life… Therein he cannot be replaced, nor can his life be repeated. Thus, everyone's task is as unique as is his specific opportunity to implement it."* So many times this specific vocation or mission plays itself out as our Passion. The first key to *Getting Where Your Need To Go* and flowing with your **LIFEFIT** is **Learning About Your Passions**.

Passion. Excitement. Enthusiasm. Zeal. Infatuation. It can be defined as intense or overpowering emotion, or intense enthusiasm. It can also be the object of your enthusiasm, like saying that music or art or dancing or counselling or developmental aid is your passion.

Human beings, by nature, are passionate beings. Love. Hate. Lust. Greed. Generosity. Warmth. Compassion. Kindness. Anger. Joy. Rage. Empathy. Sympathy. We are brimming with passions and feelings and emotions; and when we are able to align our lives with the things we are most passionate about, we will generally *Get Where We Need To Go.*

There are not many experiences that make us come alive, and fill us with energy and vitality, quite like doing the things that we are passionate about. Life feels like it has energy, significance and meaning when we exercise our passions, and when we don't exercise our passions we tend to spend a lot of time simply hoping and dreaming of the time when we can. A life devoid of living its *Passions* feels like empty and hollow existence, where all the activity, accumulations, and accomplishments don't quite fill the void.

What is interesting about our *Passions* is how intrinsic they are. We are all wired differently for different *Passions*, and it is simply "in us". We are born with built-in *Passions*, inherent *Passions*, and are basically *Passionate* about certain things, and not *Passionate* about other things.

And in this discussion, there are no right or wrong Passions. In other words, we do not have "right" passions or "wrong" *Passions*. It's about using the *Passions* that you have in order to benefit as many people as you can. We need to ensure that we only give room to healthy *Passions* in our lives, *Passions* that benefit ourselves and benefit others.

Howard Thurman said: *"Don't ask yourself what the world needs. Ask yourself what makes you come alive, and go do that, because the world needs people who have come alive!"* This thought clarifies the concept of our *Passions*... they are what makes us come alive and give us the ability to add value to the world around us. When we are alive and fully engaged, because we are living life aligned with our *Passions*, everything we do has an added extra shot of energy and abundance.

The truth is that everything in our lives flows from our *Passions* and our Heart. There is an ancient Hebrew proverb which states something to this effect: *"Guard your heart with all diligence, for from it flows the issues of life."* In the same way that none of us has the exact same rhythm in our actual physical heartbeat, we were each designed with a unique emotional *"heartbeat"* that races when we encounter situations that interest us. We instinctively feel deeply about some things and not others. Your **Passions** and motivational bent serve as an internal guidance system for your life. Your **Passions** guide what interests you and what brings you the most satisfaction and fulfilment. They motivate you to pursue certain things. There is purpose in your inborn, intrinsic, inherent interests. Your emotional heartbeat reveals keys to understanding your **LIFEFIT**. Don't ignore your natural zeal, enthusiasms, or *Passions*. *Often your calling is what unlocks your Passion.*

Passion Possibilities...

What follows is by no means an exhaustive list when it comes to *Passions*.

There are probably as many healthy *Passions* as there are people on the planet. That's what makes life so exciting. This list is meant simply to trigger some thought and possibly some self-exploration.

Art	Athletics	Singing	Technology	Videography
Music	Competition	Performing	Trades	Entrepreneurism
Design	Altruism	Drama	Building	Small Business
Politics	Generosity	Foreign Aid	Leading	Big Business
Relationships	Speaking	Driving	Managing	Exercise
Coaching	Writing	Working With The Homeless	Photography	Modelling
Counselling	Crafts	Working With Children	Physical Fitness	Working With Addictions
Creating	Culinary Arts	Finance	Social Work	Systems Analysis
Music	Technology	Family	Encouraging	Science
Agriculture	Working With The Disabled	Medical Practice	Teaching	Legal Practice
Eating	Religion	Friends	Humour	Spirituality

As I said earlier, there are probably as many healthy *Passions* as there are people on the planet. One of the best resources I have seen in this conversation is: http://www.squidoo.com/groups/whatsyourpassion.

This website asks the following:

What's your passion?

Here is your chance to share your passion with the world.

What moves you on a deep level?

Where do you find satisfaction?

Whatever it is, here's your chance to share it with others.

People post hundreds of different *Passions* there, for all the world to see. There are some unique and thoughtful *Passions* listed there, reflecting the amazing diversity of humanity.

That brings us to the next point of our conversation. How do you discover your *Passion?* And what are some crucial keys to living your *Passion?* Take the following *20-Point Passion Check*. Simply answer the questions instinctively. If you get stuck, ask those closest to you for feedback.

Discovering Your Passions

20-Point Passion Check...

What makes me glad? _____

_____

_____

What makes me sad? _____

_____

_____

What makes me mad? _____

_____

_____

What makes my heart beat faster?_____

_____

_____

If I could do anything, what would it be? _____

_____

_____

What skills come naturally to me without much thought or
effort? _____

_____

_____

What do I feel passionate about? What themes and thoughts
govern my life? _____

_____

_____

If someone asked me what my Passions are, what would I say?__

_____

_____

If I could do any job or career, what would I choose? _____

_____

_____

What energizes me? _____

_____

_____

What puts meaning and value into my life? What would I live &
possibly die for? _____

_____

_____

Where do I want to place my limited resources of time, talent
and treasure? _____

_____

_____

What types of volunteering have I done, or do I want to do?

_____

_____

_____

What types of things do people ask for my help with? _____

_____

_____

_____

In what could I become constructively obsessed? _____

_____

_____

_____

What do I love to do in my free time?_____

_____

_____

What activities, subjects, or causes have I been deeply involved
with? _____

_____

_____

What are some areas that those closest to me consider me an
expert? _____

_____

_____

When I am online, what subjects are most appealing? _____

_____

_____

What are my three big goals in life? _____

_____

_____

_____

_____

The key in any exercise like the **Passion Check** is to simply answer the questions intuitively and instinctively. If you get stuck, ask those closest to you for feedback.

Look for *threads*. Seek strands of thought and connecting lines. As you do, themes will begin to emerge. This is not a scientific process that has straight lines cognitively, but an intuitive process that draws together various components of your being, around your *Passions*. Take some time and draw some deep breaths. Listen to calming music. Get close to nature. Connect with your *Passions* on the inside. Pull the threads together. See the tapestry being woven of your *Passions*. What do you see?

My Passions:

_____

_____

_____

_____

_____

Keys To Living Your P.A.S.S.I.O.N. ...

P – **Pursuit** – To live our *Passions*, we have to make a clear and determined choice to PURSUE them. We need to pursue our *Passions*, to go after them with energy and vitality and priority. Terri Guillemets said:

"Chase down your passion like it's the last bus of the night."

A – **Ask Questions** – Continually ask questions, research, and draw on the knowledge and wisdom of others as you pursue your passion. This is about working *smart* to fulfill your *Passions*, not just working *hard*. As in any area of life, *Passion,* without wisdom and knowledge, is dangerous!

S – **Seek** *Partners* – The fulfilment of your *Passions* was never meant to be a solo project. Look for partners when you seek to fulfill your *Passions*, partners who will challenge, inspire and encourage you. People who tear down your *Passions* and are a negative influence should be avoided. We need all the support we can get as we pursue our *Passions*. We can do far more when we partner with others than we can alone.

S – *Strategize* **& Plan** – Take some time to create an action plan around how you will actually take your *Passion* and bring it into practical life. So many people fail here, because in the end, living your *Passions* is about planning, prioritizing, and discipline. Don't neglect these crucial keys.

I – *Introspection* – We all get distracted at times. People who live their *Passion*, and experience the buzz that living their *Passion* brings, simply get less distracted than others. Regularly check yourself to ensure you are living in alignment with your *Passions*. We can't afford to allow the pursuit of the everyday to pull us away from the exceptional.

O – *Own* It – So many people never pursue their *Passions* because they do not exhibit ownership, i.e., they blame other people and circumstances for holding them back from living a *Passion-Focused* life. We need to own fulfilling our *Passions*. At the end of our days, we need to know in our hearts that we took responsibility and owned our *Passions*.

N – *Never* **Quit** – This one is simple. We need to be undeterred and not easily discouraged as we recklessly live our Passions. Don't give up! The truth is that if we *follow our Passion, success will follow us!*

Georg Wilhelm Friedrich Hegel said about our *Passions*: *"Nothing great in the world has been accomplished without passion."* Let's pursue our *Passions*.

Getting Where You Need To Go
Chapter 5 – *"I"* –
Investigating Your Personality

Getting Where Your Need To Go is first about **Learning About Your Passions**, and then about **Investigating Your Personality**. The second key to *Getting Where Your Need To Go* and flowing with your **LIFEFIT** is **Investigating Your Personality**. The reason the word "investigating" is used here is because learning about yourself, and your uniqueness, is a journey of discovery. It is something that doesn't happen overnight. It occurs as we explore and unearth all the wonders of our distinctive *Personality*.

You just need to Google the word *"Personality"* to see there is an abundance of active discussion and many theories around *Personality*, and *Personality* types. My main hope here is not to be an exhaustive reference guide for the field of human *Personality*, but to simply make a passionate argument that to *Get Where We Need To Go*, we need to flow and live aligned with our unique and distinctive *Personality*.

Personality can be described as somebody's set of characteristics, the distinguishing characteristics of an individual, their uniqueness. It is what makes *"you"* you. In essence, it is the sum of a person's interests, attitudes, emotional responses, behavioural patterns, or other individual traits that make a person who they are. Your *Personality* is your specific persona, your qualities, your individualism, your uniqueness. It is what makes you one of a kind, and what makes you exceptional. It is your *distinctiveness*. Charles Schwab perhaps said it best when he noted, *"Personality is to a man what perfume is to a flower."* Norman O. Brown said about *Personality: "I am what is mine. Personality is the original personal property."* [23]

See, there was no cookie cutter present when we were designed and when we were birthed. Nature loves variety. Nature

---

[23] Both quotes found on
http://www.worldofquotes.com/topic/Personality/1/index.html

made introverts and extroverts; people who love routine and those who love variety. Some of us are *"thinkers"*, others are *"feelers"*, and others are visual and so they are *"seers"*. Some work best individually, and some work best with a team.

Your *Personality* is your unique "ME"; that which makes you, you. *It is the "who" in your "you"*. Your *Personality* affects how and where you use everything else: your passions, gifts, abilities, education, training, calling, and all else. It's easier to work with the grain than against it. When you are forced to function in a manner that is out of sync with your *Personality*, it creates stress, tension, and discomfort; requires extra exertion and energy; and produces far less meaningful results. You were made to be You! When you live consistent with your *Personality*, you experience fulfilment, effectiveness, and fruitfulness. It feels good when you are in alignment with what you were made you to be.

Every flavour of *Personality* is equally effective. There is no *"right"* or *"wrong"* *Personality*. We need all kinds of *Personalities* to balance and give flavour to life, relationships, business, and the world. The question is not one of a *"right"* or *"wrong"* *Personality*, but of living in a way that flows with your unique **LIFEFIT**. *Getting Where Your Need To Go* is about living and thinking and relating and working in a way that is in alignment with your *Personality*. Maximum effectiveness for each one of us is achieved when we live in a way that is congruent with our inherent *Personality*. This brings success and joy.

Different Personality Styles

As I mentioned earlier, Google lists hundred of thousands of reference points for the word *"Personality"*, theories around *Personality*, and *Personality* types. There are many different perspectives when it comes to *Personality*, but there seems to be broad agreement that to *Get Where We Need To Go*, we need to flow and live aligned with our unique and distinctive *Personality*.

See, enthusiasm is one of the most powerful engines of success. When we do a thing, we need to do it with all our mind, with all our heart and strength and will and effort; to put our whole soul into it. Nothing great was ever achieved without enthusiasm. This flows organically when we stamp it with our own *Personality*. We will be naturally active, energetic, and enthusiastic when we engage our *Personality*.

Here I'll share my personal take on different *Personality Styles*. As I have counselled and coached over the years, I have observed broad themes or types, or even different "brands" of *Personalities*. These are not meant to be hard definitions that box us in, but descriptive concepts that serve to help us define some sort of *Personality* and individual characteristics. As you read through the following list, don't try to identify yourself exclusively with one type of *Personality*. Know that many of us have characteristics of many different *Personalities* at different moments in our lives, and that we're continuing to evolve and grow as people. Look for threads which could reveal your *Personality*, which if woven together may present a complete picture.

The picture we are looking for is one of *orientation*. It is not so much about how a person *acts* in every situation, but how they are oriented to react and respond generally. All of us come to life with an internal driving force, a sense of how it feels natural for us to simply be. This is our *Personality*. The following *Personality Styles* have simple, though not extensive descriptions.

Feeler – *Feelers* literally feel their way through life. We all feel our way through life, but *Feelers* tend to have a more accurate antenna, the ability to be more sensitive, perceptive, and aware because their "sensor" functions better than the rest of us. In photography, different cameras have differently sized sensors. Sensors in a camera simply read the information (i.e. light, color, depth of field, etc.) that is available in any given image. So, generally speaking, if the sensor on a camera is larger, it has the capacity to read and capture more information, leading to a much higher image quality. In the same way, *Feelers* simply sense and

66

read and capture more of the information in given situations, thus reflecting more feeling and more emotion. Being a *Feeler* is amazing because the emotions are richer, the perceptions are deeper, and the experiences are more profound. They are kinesthetic, and continually feel more of a situation than others, and thus carry intense emotion. The orientation of the *Feeler* is simply to feel. This manifests itself in empathy, sympathy, compassion, care, tenderness, and the ability to listen, comfort and show kindness.

Seer – *Seers* also have a larger "sensor" than the rest of us. The difference is that they tend to picture it rather than feel it. They would be described as visual people, people who tend to think in terms of pictures and images and perceptions and illustrations. They often don't want information relayed conceptually, but in picture format so they can view the image in a way that makes sense for them. They also tend to be intuitive and imaginative, sometimes even seeing things or picturing them before they happen as part of their planning process. *Seers* love pictures, graphs, charts, and imagery. Being a *Seer* is extraordinary, because generally, what they see is not one dimensional, and black and white; it is three dimensional, rich in colour, shape, detail, and vivid imagery. The orientation of the *Seer* is simply to see, perceive, and visualize.

Thinker – *Thinkers* tend to be just that: logical, grounded, and linear in their thought process and orientation. They love spreadsheets, lists, reading and reference material, and detailed analysis. *Thinkers* prefer response over reaction, evaluation over execution, and analysis over action. However, once a decision has been made, founded upon research and data analysis, a *Thinker* is almost unmovable in terms of conviction or in terms of obstacle to that decision. The orientation of the *Thinker* is simply to think; to logically reason and weigh out the issues at hand before a course of action is decided upon. The beauty of a *Thinker* is their keen ability to evaluate and assess a thing, based not on feeling, but on sharp analysis and keen investigation.

Doer – *Doers* are action-based people. While the *Thinker* is pondering, the *Seer* is envisioning, and the *Feeler* is sensing, the *Doer* has already made plans and is in the middle of getting it done. *Doers* love activity, movement, momentum, and achievement. They rarely get stuck in the paralysis of analysis. Van Gough said, *"Great things are done by a series of small things brought together".* *Doers* intuitively understand this, knowing that nothing gets done until it gets done, and so they simply *"go after it".* *Doers* are unhindered by needing to know every fact and small detail. They are satisfied when they have a sense of the big picture which gives them guidance around what to do. *Doers* in their finest state get things done, and get them done with an efficiency and quality bordering on perfection. If you are building anything, you need some *Doers*.

Planter – *Planters* tend to be those who dream, initiate, plan and then execute, all in a short period of time. They tend to be creative thinkers who aren't often confined to a narrow field of view in terms of how it has always been done or what can be done in a given context. They see possibilities, solutions, and opportunities, and are instinctively able to re-frame the norms in terms of *"what can be".* George Bernard Shaw said: *"All progress is initiated by challenging current conceptions, and executed by supplanting existing institutions".* People who are bent mainly towards conservative values and stability may read a statement like that and go into cardiac arrest. *Planters* read it and assume everyone naturally agrees. Nido Qubein said, *"The greatest enemy of your creative powers is smug complacency – being satisfied with less than what you are capable of doing"* [24]. *Planters* don't get complacent, but inherently drive for change, improvement,

---

[24] Glenn Van Ekeren, *Speaker's Sourcebook II:* 1994: Prentice Hall, Paramus, New Jersey, p.80

advancement and progress every step of the way. This infuses *Planters* with strong creativity, high energy levels, and the power to initiate, plan, and execute, and then move on to the next thing, project, obstacle or dream.

Builder – *Builders* tend to take a long-term view of things. Whatever they do, they do it with a far-reaching solution in mind. Being a *Builder* is an orientation that describes a person who is philosophically opposed to band-aid solutions, quick fixes, and short term remedies. This attitude changes everything because rather than wanting to just *"grease the squeaky wheel"*, *Builders* like to fix the whole bike. Robert Reich described it like this: *"A leader is someone who steps back from the entire system and tries to build a more collaborative, more innovative system that will work over the long term"* [25]. It could be said that short-term thinking leads to narrow thinking, faulty remedies, and incomplete solutions. *Builders* seek to avoid this at all costs. The following words could generally describe *Builders:* thorough, methodical, systematic, meticulous, detailed, complete, consistent, careful, total.

Leader – Much has been written and said about *Leaders*, but when we talk about *Leaders* from a *Personality* perspective, we are speaking not so much about developing the skill of leadership, and certainly not about a leadership position, but being born with the orientation, mindset, attitude and *Personality* of a *Leader*. *Leaders* are those who love to be out in front, who enjoy taking charge, who paint a clear picture of the destination and motivate the group to go there. They are inspiring, challenging, encouraging, and stirring. They have the capacity to unlock the potential of a person or a group, and inspire them to enjoy full abundance. They are often focused on the big picture, and are not so much focused on what is, but on what can be. They see things, not so much as they are, but as they are meant to be. Thus *Leaders*

---

[25] http://thinkexist.com/quotes/with/keyword/long-term/

by *Personality* take us somewhere. Henry Kissinger said, *"The task of a leader is to get his people from where they are to where they have not been"*. Those with the *Personality* of a *Leader* do this inherently: instinctive intentional influence.

Manager – Once again, here we refer not to a position of management but to the orientation and *Personality* of a *Manager*. *Managers* above all thrive on organization, structure and form. They generally perform in a consistent and predictable manner, and are often described by those around them as consistent, detail-oriented, and preferring policy and procedure to interaction and relational engagement. *Managers* thrive in a structured and regulated environment, and tend to be the ones who bring order out of chaos for others. While the *Leader* sees the big picture and takes the group in that direction, the *Manager* is the one who plans the individual steps of the journey. The *Leader* may have a clear grasp of where the group needs to go, but often is not clear on the logistics, details and particulars of actually getting the group there. This is where *Managers* come in. *Managers* intuitively seem to grasp where the ends need to be tied together, where the gaps are, and are skilled at pulling it all together, grasping and organizing all the component parts. Without *Managers*, groups and organizations can survive, but will struggle to thrive and reach their full potential.

Dreamer – The best way to describe *Dreamers* is with the word *"imaginative"*. *Dreamers* are out of the box, creative people who are often artistic, inventive, even inspired, and tend to have a different way of approaching problems and challenges. While the *Leader* is busy seeing the big picture, the *Manager* is organizing the team and resources, to get them there, and the *Doer* is busy getting it done, the *Dreamer* is wondering if we need to get there at all, and if there is perhaps not a better place to go, a better way to get there, and a better reason why. *Dreamers* are often guided by a strong sense of justice, right and wrong, and fairness, and so they tend to view the world, people, systems, and structures through that prism. Perhaps the best example of a modern day *Dreamer* would be Martin Luther King, Jr., and not just because of his famous *"I Have A Dream"* speech. King viewed the world differently, and asked questions that those around him were afraid to ask; questions he gave others permission to repeat because of his bold and fearless approach. King asked questions of justice, of fairness, of equality, of respect. *Dreamers* often ask these kinds of value-based questions, and ask them in an imaginative, inspired, and even artistic way. However, not every *Dreamer* dreams in the field of social justice, and so *Dreamers* tend to dream in the realm of their *Passion*.

Server – *Servers* have an attitude and orientation to serve. It makes them feel alive. We all serve, and serving others is key to relational and career success. However, for those wired with the *Personality* of a *Server*, serving is their *Passion*. They have a deep-seated desire to make the lives of others easier, more convenient, and more enjoyable. Rather than leading, directing or managing, *Servers* love to facilitate, assist, and make the journey of others more palatable. Kevin Eikenberry said this, and it describes the orientation of a *Server: "The simple act of helping someone—with no desire (or possibility) of repayment is good for us and our self-image, and it may positively change the life or outlook of the receiver for the day!"* [26] That is exactly the way *Servers* think and feel when they approach life, relationships, and work. They inherently want to be the background support mechanism that causes it to all come together. *Servers* find genuine joy in volunteering and other supportive capacities.

Comforter – The *Personality* of a *Comforter* is perfectly described with the word *Comfort*. They genuinely care about others, and will go to extraordinary lengths to show authentic care, real concern, and true reassurance. For them, life is not measured

---

[26] http://www.myfavoriteezines.com/ezinedirectory/quotes-about-service-serving.html

in accomplishments or achievements, but in the moments when they know they have reached out and touched others in fearful, stressed, anxious places, and made life better for them. Instinctively, they realize they may not be able to change the person's situation or circumstance, but if they can brighten their day and re-frame their perspective, they will make a difference. The orientation of a Comforter is to encourage, to lift, and to cheer.

Healer – *Healers* are all about standing in the gap, salving the pain, and healing the wound. While others might be content to let the mentally and emotionally wounded simply "tough it out", *Healers* want to see them enjoy a place of health, wholeness, and abundance. *Healers* instinctively want to nurture, nourish, look after, care for and authentically bring people to a place of well-being. It is how they are oriented and wired. They are skilled at not only identifying the root of a person's dysfunction, but also knowing how to close the gap between their pain and dysfunction, and their mental/emotional health. Often *Healers* go into professions and careers involving medicine, social work, and mental/emotional health.

What Is My Personality?

The list above is not designed to be exhaustive. Because every person is so wonderfully unique, there are probably as many different Personality Types as there are people. We simply need to look at the diversity and multiplicity of nature to see that we could all add to this list.

Sometimes when people read lists of *Personality Types*, they get caught up trying to definitely determine their *Personality Type*. Don't get too hung up on that. However, it is likely that we tend toward one or two *Personality Types* more than others. Here are a few simple keys in this journey of self-discovery:

Look For Resonance – As you read the list above, don't try to identify yourself exclusively with one only, but realize that many of us have characteristics of many different **Personalities** at different moments in our lives, and that we're also continuing to evolve and grow as people. Look for threads that reveal your *Personality*, which if woven together present a complete picture. As you scan the list, look for *resonance.* What sits right with you? What feels right? What just seems like it fits?

Look For Relationships – What do the people around you say? Ask the 3 or 4 people who are closest to you to read the list above, and then ask them what one or two *Personality Types* best fit you. Generally, people who know us well have an accurate perspective.

Look For Results – When you flow in one or more of the *Personality Types* above, what results do you experience? The proving is always in the doing. If you think your *Personality Type* is that of a *Doer*, and yet you want to be involved a lot more in the planning and strategy side, you might be more of a *Manager*. If you think you should be a *Leader* and yet it feels much more natural to *Serve*, then perhaps that is what you should be. Go with the flow when it comes to results, especially with *Personality Types*.

Incorporating Your Personality Into Daily Life

The key in this conversation of *Personality* as it pertains to *Getting Where You Need To Go* is this: **Living Your LIFEFIT.** We need to **live** our **LIFEFIT**. In other words, we need to live and flow in a way that is aligned and congruent with our **LIFEFIT**.

If we are truly living our **LIFEFIT**, our *Personality* will have a huge bearing on the expression of the following:

Our Values – Our values are influenced and to some degree even balanced by our *Personality*. Values devoid of *Personality* can be perceived as cold, heartless and almost without meaning. Express your values in a way that flows with your *Personality*.

Our Emotions – Our emotions are often shaped and influenced by our *Personality*, and the key is in finding balance, so we are not blaming emotional outbursts and/or a lack of emotional control on our *Personality*.

Find healthy ways emotionally of expressing your *Personality*.

Our Relationships – Relationships are often formed through *Personality* connections, and can just as easily be broken through *Personality*. Look for friendships and partners that compliment your *Personality*.

Our Spirituality – People's expression of their spirituality is often influenced and formed by their *Personality*. When a person's *Personality* flows with their spirituality, it is a wonderful, peaceful combination.

Our Work – Working in a job or career that is not congruent with your *Personality* is painful, both for you and for those who have to work with you. In planning your career and roles in any given field, take the time to look at your *Personality* and ensure a proper fit.

Our Passions – Earlier, I said: *"...Dreamers tend to dream in the realm of their Passion."* This is key. We will express our *Personality* in the realm of our *Passion*. Maybe it is simpler to say that as we pursue our *Passions*, we will do so in a way that aligns with our *Personality*. Give yourself time and space to do this, because it will lead to a greater level of personal satisfaction as you pursue your *Passions*.

Resources re: Personality

This is by no means exhaustive, but here is a listing of some resources around the discussion of human *Personality*, different *Personality* types, and some useful tests for locating your unique *Personality*. In no way am I issuing a blanket endorsement for everything on the individual sites, but they all give some basis for exploring this area. Some have a cost attached to them, but most are free and offer some perspective on the area of *Personality*.

http://www.personalitypathways.com/type_inventory.html

http://www.personalitypage.com/portraits.html

http://www.psychometrics.com/en-us/assessments.htm?gclid=CLOTlfutr6ICFRCfnAodO2LQSQ

http://www.personalitypage.com/

http://www.9types.com/

http://www.mypersonality.info/personality-types/

http://www.humanmetrics.com/cgi-win/jtypes2.asp

http://www.outofservice.com/bigfive/

As we conclude this chapter, once again, the key is **Living Your LIFEFIT**. We need to **LIVE** our **LIFEFIT**. In other words, we need to live and flow in a way that is aligned and congruent with our **LIFEFIT**. Live in a way that flows with your unique *Personality*. It will lead to greater fulfilment, personal satisfaction, and effectiveness in the long term. Don't deny or suppress your *Personality*, instead, properly flow with and express it!

Getting Where You Need To Go
Chapter 6 – "F" –
Finding Out Your Gifts & Abilities

Getting Where Your Need To Go is first about Learning About Your **Passions**, and then about Investigating Your **Personality**. The third key to *Getting Where Your Need To Go* and flowing with your **LIFEFIT** is Finding Out Your *Gifts & Abilities*. I use the phrase "finding out" your *Gifts & Abilities* because learning about yourself, and your *Gifts & Abilities*, is a journey of discovery. It is something that doesn't happen overnight. It occurs as we explore and unearth all the wonders of our amazing *Gifts & Abilities*.

Human beings, as a whole, are enormously talented and spectacularly gifted. The challenge is not to be gifted, because all of us are, but to find out our gifts, talents, and abilities, and then to put them to work. As Markus Buckingham said in Now Discover Your Strengths: *"The real tragedy of life is not that each of us doesn't have enough strengths, it's that we fail to see the ones we have"* [27]. The key to success and fulfilment in life is **Living Your LIFEFIT**. In other words, we need to live in a way that is congruent and harmonious with our **LIFEFIT**. We need to flow with our *Gifts & Abilities*. This leads to greater fulfilment, personal satisfaction, and effectiveness in the long term. Don't deny your *Gifts & Abilities*, but flow with and express them. This guarantees the things you touch will turn to gold!

John Wooden, who was perhaps the most effective coach in basketball history, and who definitely used his *Gifts & Abilities*, winning 10 NCAA Championships as a coach, said when it comes to using your *Gifts & Abilities*: *"Don't measure yourself by what you have accomplished, but by what you should have accomplished with your ability."* [28] So many of us measure ourselves by what we have accomplished, or even worse, by the accomplishments of others. Sometimes, we even measure

---

[27] Markus Buckingham and Donald Clifton, *Now Discover Your Strengths*, 1991: The Free Press, Toronto, p.12

[28] http://quotations.about.com/od/abilityquotes/a/ability1.htm

ourselves by the pressure and expectations of others. We need to take a detailed look at what we can and should accomplish with our specific *Gifts & Abilities*, and go after that with all our heart, soul, mind, and strength.

There is an anecdote of a chief executive who was going away on a journey. We're not sure if this trip was business or pleasure, but I guess that's not the point. The point is that at the moment of her departure, she called her executive team into the board room and had a key conversation.

This conversation involved the allocation of specific assets to particular board members while she was gone, and the assignment of specific responsibilities to each one until she returned. Different assets were given to different board members based on their ability to handle them. Different responsibilities were given to different people based on their level of expertise.

To one board member, responsibility was given over 10 departments of the business. To another, responsibility was given over 5 departments. To another, responsibility was given over 1 department of the business. Though the 3rd person was only given one department, it was a key department, and one that could drive significant profit. When everything had been properly delegated and duly assigned, the CEO went on her trip, with the anticipation that while she was gone, expectations would be met, responsibilities would be fulfilled, and assets would grow. The clear goal was not only *maintenance*, but *increase* in each department and assignment.

While she was gone, the one assigned 10 departments went to work diligently, facing the challenges and obstacles along the way, and generally executed with excellence. While the CEO was gone, he doubled revenue and profit in his 10 departments. Job well done.

The employee who was assigned 5 departments also went to work. She had not been given 10 departments like her co-worker, but nonetheless treated the responsibility with the same care and diligence. In some ways, having a little less turned out to be an advantage, because her focal point was quite narrow, and results came quickly due to hard work, pushing through difficulties and hindrances, and some good fortune which came her way. She also doubled revenue and profit in all 5 departments.

The employee given 1 department was a bit of a contrast. He was the sort of person who spent a lot of time comparing his positions and titles to others, and was either inflated or deflated by that. When the CEO left and he was only assigned 1 department, he was discouraged and took it as an insult. Not only that, but he was a person who was averse to taking a risk, working hard, and simply using what he had been given. He was always looking for the *"perfect opportunity"*, and he allowed this to hold him back when he didn't see the *"perfect opportunity"* right there in front of him.

So, he sat on his department, not *losing* ground, revenue, or profit; but not *gaining* anything either. His disappointment and deflation, which came as a result of comparing himself to others, and his fear of loss, risk, and hard work, all combined to keep his department in maintenance mode. While the CEO was gone, his department did not move ahead at all.

Several months later, the CEO returned. The one who had been assigned 10 departments, and the one assigned 5 departments, had fulfilled their delegated responsibilities, doubling their assets, revenue, and profit. Praise, recognition, and promotion immediately followed. They were set for life, because they had utilized what they had been given to the fullest extent.

The CEO also reviewed the one assigned the single department. He had allowed discouragement, fear, laziness, the perceived lack of the *"perfect opportunity"*, and risk aversion to lock him into a maintenance mode. The CEO had been clear in terms of the expectations of increase, fully using what had been given, and delivering profit. This department head was demoted immediately, and relieved of duty. Sadly, he blamed the CEO and her initial delegation to him of only one department as the cause.

This small parable reveals several key truths when it comes to our *Gifts & Abilities...* what I call, **"10 Key Principles About Potential"**.

10 Key Principles About Potential...

1. There Is A Sense In Which Each of Us Has Been *"Called"* – The CEO *called* each department head and assigned them specific tasks. There is a sense in which you and I have been *"called"* to use our *Gifts & Abilities*; there is almost a divine or sacred sense of duty when it comes to us using our *Gifts & Abilities* and putting them to work. They are a huge key to our own success and fulfilment. Without using our *Gifts & Abilities*, our chances at success are very small. George Bernard Shaw succinctly expressed this when he said: *"Martyrdom is the only way in which a man can become famous without ability."* [29]

2. We Have All Been Blessed With *Gifts & Abilities* – Every single one of us has been blessed and honoured with unique *Gifts & Abilities*. Talents have been distributed throughout the whole of the human race. I am constantly amazed by the *Gifts & Abilities* of people; especially those that don't appear on the surface to have a lot, but in fact do! Lawrence Welk said this for all of us: *"To be granted some kind of usable talent and to be able to use it to the fullest extent of which you are capable – this, to me, is a kind of joy that is almost unequalled"*.

3. We've Been Given Different *Gifts & Abilities* – Though we're all empowered with some significant *Gifts & Abilities*, we were each given *different Gifts & Abilities*. This should be celebrated! While some spend much of their time wondering why they did not receive what someone else received in terms of *Gifts & Abilities*, effective people are too busy working with what they have, growing into success! Your focus and attention span is too important to divert it onto what you don't have. Red Auerbach, another great basketball coach, said: *"Just do what you do best"*.

4. We Are Not In Control Of What We Have Been Given, Only What We Do With What We Have Been Given – One of

---

[29] http://quotations.about.com/od/abilityquotes/a/ability1.htm

the crucial keys to life vitality and contentment is t[...]
controllables, and don't sweat what you cannot contr[...]
control in regard to *Gifts & Abilities* is what we do [...]
have been given. We can't control what we have b[...]
don't spend lots of time thinking about it. It's counter[...]

5. *Gifts & Abilities* **Are Tools** – When we discover our *Gifts & Abilities*, we come a long way to discovering our **LIFEFIT**. There are quite a few insightful resources in the marketplace today about our *Gifts & Abilities*, our talents, and our strengths. I encourage you to become an avid reader of these because there is probably no one perspective on this topic which is 100% comprehensive. However, "Now, Discover Your Strengths", by Marcus Buckingham, is surely one of the finest. Not only has he done extensive research on this topic from a sociological perspective, but also he lists many different types of strengths and defines our strengths quite clearly. For our purposes here however, I simply define *Gifts & Abilities* as tools. Every task needs the right tools, and we have all been given certain tools to accomplish certain tasks: our *Gifts & Abilities*. *Gifts & Abilities* can be described as the *tools* we have been given to fulfill the *tasks* we need to do. They are our **Natural Endowments**. The truth is, when we are good at something, we feel good doing it and have success in it. That is what an old saying tells us: *A person's gift promotes him, and makes room for him.*

6. We Need To Put Our *Gifts & Abilities* **To Work** – The happiest people in life are the busiest people… not just busy doing anything anywhere with anyone, but busy doing what they were designed to do, what they were born to do, in terms of their *Gifts & Abilities*. Some wait for the perfect opportunity; others wait to be paid and compensated. My best advice is to simply get busy using your *Gifts & Abilities*. Put to work what you have been given in terms of your *Gifts & Abilities*. Vaclav Havel, who helped lead Czechoslovakia out of Communism, said this in support of just doing it: *"It is not enough to stare up the steps, we must step up the stairs"*. Step up the stairs by working what you have been given!

7. If You Use What You Have, You Will Increase It – We e born to use the tools we have! We need to put our *Gifts & Abilities* to work, and as we do, they grow. In other words, we get better at them, and we also get more comfortable with them. See, *Every Tool Is Meant To Be Grown Into*. We need to give ourselves time to get comfortable with our *Gifts & Abilities*. It takes time! And, *every tool is meant to be regularly sharpened*. Just because you are good at something, doesn't mean you can't get better. Using your *Gifts & Abilities* helps to increase them, helps you to feel more comfortable as you use them, and helps you sharpen them as well.

8. The Fulfilment Is Not Just In Maintenance, But In Increase – In the spheres of business and life, maintenance is the bar set by those who value survival above all else. This is a way of thinking that is not so much concerned with leaving a positive footprint and making a difference, but simply getting by. Dreams do not come true, nor is true inherent personal fulfilment realized when *maintenance* is the mentality. We need to constantly challenge ourselves towards *increase*, *growth* and *more* if we want to fulfill our true potential. Using our *Gifts & Abilities* to their full extent is key.

9. Hindrances To Using Our Gifts & Abilities Include:

- ***Discouragement*** - Lou Holtz said, *"Ability is what you're capable of doing. Motivation determines what you do. Attitude determines how well you do it"*. When we compare our Gifts & Abilities to the Gifts & Abilities of others, we are naturally discouraged and deflated, and de-motivated, because there'll always be someone we perceive to be "better" than ourselves. Be very cautious when it comes to comparing yourself to others, because it generally leads to either inflation or deflation of the ego, which is never healthy! Have courage enough to stand and realize that you are a uniquely engineered, specifically designed, one-of-a-kind, tailor-made human being who is different and diverse, and celebrate that. You are you!

- *Fear* – Fear of failure, fear of the unknown, fear of not measuring up, fear of being seen, fear of people, fear of change, fear of new things. Many fears can hold us back from using our *Gifts & Abilities* for others. Robin Sharma said, *"Fear is nothing more than a mental monster you have created, a negative stream of consciousness".* This is so true. There is a freedom that comes when we make a conscious choice to move beyond our fears, and to overcome them. When fear is what holds you back, which is this negative energy, it takes the positive energy of faith, hope and healthy choices to overcome it. If successful people have one common trait, it's an utter lack of cynicism. The world owes them nothing. The world doesn't frighten them. They go out and find what they need without asking for permission; they're driven, talented, and work through negatives by focusing on the positives.

- *Laziness* – There is a principle that goes like this: *"Pay now, play later. Or, you can play now, but you will pay later".* In other words, we are all going to have *pay* at some point. Some are simply lazy and want to *play* now instead of *paying* now. Others are wise and *pay* now, because in essence, they are booking a play date for themselves in the future. History gives example of those who did not use their *Gifts & Abilities* to their fullest extent because of laziness. Laziness is a cancer which diminishes our *Gifts & Abilities.* Zig Ziglar said: *"You are the only one who can use your ability. It is an awesome responsibility."* [30] It's a responsibility we will forever regret if we don't fulfill it. Work it!

- *Looking For The "Perfect Opportunity"* – I once had a good friend who is extremely talented, very intelligent, and liked by almost everyone he meets. He is probably still a friend, but we haven't had the opportunity to connect for a number of years. He was the guy I always envied, the guy who everyone liked, everyone respected, and everyone saw the potential in. It

---

[30] http://quotations.about.com/od/abilityquotes/a/ability1.htm

seemed as though everyone expected amazing things from him, and he also expected amazing things from himself. However, from what I can gather, he has not attained much of what he used to dream about. He was hit with some tragedy at an early age, tragedy that would be enough to give anyone pause, but not the kind of tragedy that would destroy a person's heart. However, though his heart was not destroyed, something shifted in terms of his perspective and how he saw the world. He became much more cautious, much more careful, much more analytical. He didn't seem to want to step out anymore and always looked for the *"Perfect Opportunity"*. He needed to see Michael Jordan in Nike's **"Failure"** commercial. In it, Jordan says, *"I've missed more than 9,000 shots in my career. I've lost almost 300 games. 26 times I've been trusted to take the game winning shot and missed. I've failed over and over and over again in my life. And that is why I succeed."* [31] Wow. Could you imagine if Michael Jordan had always looked for the *"Perfect Opportunity"* while he was a basketball player? Imagine if he was held back by the false belief that there ever is an actual *"Perfect Opportunity"*? All the artistry we saw from him over his perennial all-star, championship career would have been lost as he sat and analyzed situation after situation, looking for that *"Perfect Opportunity"*. It does not exist, so please don't wait for it!

- ***Risk Aversion*** – Like looking for the *"Perfect Opportunity"*, an aversion to risk can hold you back. People don't want to lay it on the line because of fear of loss, fear of failure, and fear of having nothing left. To *Get Where We Need To Go* and use our *Gifts & Abilities* to their fullest extent, we need to get over it. We need to be averse to risk aversion, and recognize that if there is nothing ventured, probably nothing will be gained. If we invest nothing, probably no investments will grow. If we don't sow seed, we will probably not see a harvest. Elbert Hubbard said, *"The greatest mistake you can make in life is to*

---

[31] http://www.youtube.com/watch?v=45mMioJ5szc

be continually fearing you will make one." Using your *Gifts &* *Abilities* takes risk, and it takes stepping out of our comfortable places. When you feel a reluctance to take a risk coming on, simply deny it and use your *Gifts & Abilities* 110%! I love this quote by super-salesman Jeffrey Gitomer: *"Obstacles can't stop you. Problems can't stop you. Most of all, other people can't stop you. Only you can stop you."*

10. We Find Satisfaction & Success As We Use Our *Gifts & Abilities* – Never hide what you have been given in terms of *Gifts & Abilities!* There is far more in you than you have let out up until now. Richard E. Boyd said, *"Few men during their lifetime come anywhere near exhausting the resources within them. There are deep wells of strength that are seldom used."* The only way these *deep wells of strength* get utilized is through exploring and then using our *Gifts & Abilities* to their full potential. This is crucial because *under-utilized potential always results in poverty*: first of mind, then emotion, spirit, and body. Eventually, even financial poverty. An ancient proverb tells us, *"Much food is in the fallow ground of the poor...".* Certainly, not *all* poverty is due to not exploring and using your potential. But *some* is. Poverty is much more than money. It is also *spiritual, mental, relational, occupational, emotional,* and many other aspects of our lives. Not using our potential leads to the greatest poverty of all: *"Could have been...".* Fallow ground is un-cultivated land, land that has not been used. In the ground of the poor, there is "much food". This food is locked up in the ground because the ground has not been cultivated or developed. In the same way, we need to cultivate and develop our *Gifts & Abilities.*

In this conversation about *Gifts & Abilities*, we need to remember that *Every Tool Is Meant To Be Used With Other Tools.* In other words, don't try to get the job done alone. The job is meant to be so big that your tools alone, your *Gifts & Abilities* alone, will not get the job done. So, we need to create *partnerships. Strategic alliances. Teams.* Even the Lone Ranger had Tonto.

84

This concept of teaming up to use our *Gifts & Abilities* speaks to humility. *Humility Is Crucial As We Use Our Tools; our Gifts & Abilities*. There is an ancient Chinese proverb that reminds us of the value of humility: *"Behind every able man and woman, there are always other able men and women."* In other words, no one is able to do alone what another can do with partners.

As we conclude this chapter, the key is **Living Your LIFEFIT**. We need to **LIVE** our **LIFEFIT**! In other words, we need to live and flow in a way that is aligned and congruent with our **LIFEFIT**. Live in a way that flows with your unique *Gifts & Abilities*. It will lead to greater fulfilment, personal satisfaction, and effectiveness in the long term. Don't be held back. After all, as Thomas Carlyle, the Scottish philosopher and author, said: *"The king is the man who can."* Be a king! Be a queen! In the words of Johnny Depp in the movie "Once Upon A Time In Mexico": *"Are you a Mexi-CAN, or a Mexi-CAN'T?"* Be a "can-do" kind of person!

Getting Where You Need To Go
Chapter 7 – "E" –
Exploring & Clarifying Your Mission

Getting Where Your Need To Go is first about **<u>Learning</u> About Your Passions**, and then about **Investigating Your Personality**. The third key to flowing with your **LIFEFIT** is **Finding Out Your Gifts & Abilities**. Next, to *Get Where You Need To Go*, you need to **Explore & Clarify Your Mission**. We all need to allow room for our sense of personal calling to breathe, evolve, and take shape. As Po Bronson said in, "What Should I Do With My Life?":

> *"We are all writing the story of our life. We want to know what it's "about", what are its themes and which theme is on the rise. We demand of it something deeper, or richer, or more substantive. We want to know where we're headed – not to spoil our own ending by ruining the surprise, but we want to ensure that when the ending comes, it won't be shallow. We will have done something. We will not have squandered our time here."* [32]

For some, when I have taught this before, the question has risen: *Why Place Exploring & Clarifying Your Mission or Calling here, and not at the start of your* **LIFEFIT?** The best answer I can offer is that we need to learn some other things about ourselves before we create a Personal Mission Statement. Too many rush to create a Personal Mission Statement without taking time to unearth and explore their *Passions, Personality* and *Gifts & Abilities*. They don't take the time to weave them all together into some sort of tapestry with congruence, symmetry and shape. So they don't really know themselves, and what makes them tick. It's

---

[32] Po Bronson, *What Should I Do With My Life?* Random House, Toronto 2002: p.xiii

for that reason, I have placed the piece about *Exploring & Clarifying Our Mission* here.

Exploring & Clarifying Our Mission is, in essence, the very theme and central thought of this book. That stream of thought, and stream of consciousness, states that, fundamentally, we are not simply the random collection of cells, tissue, and fibre, but that each and every one of us has a unique and specific purpose. Each one of us was placed on this planet for a specific *reason*, a specific *purpose*, a specific *mission*, and thus have inherent *value*. We can sum this Mission up with a Personal Mission Statement that doesn't limit our Mission but exposes it, expands it, and gives us a clear target.

Peter Drucker, the great management guru, said: *"There is nothing so useless as doing efficiently that which should not be done at all."* [33] See, this is the tragedy of our modern age. We are often busy climbing ladders very quickly and very efficiently, only to realize when we get to the top, that they are leaning against the wrong building. At that point, having missed out on our *Personal Mission*, we experience the pain of regret and missed opportunity. For sure, we can set our ladder up against another building, but is it too late? I have often heard it said that the saddest two words in the English language are: *"If only"*. I could only add to that three words: *"Should have been…"*

Albert Schweitzer said, *"The tragedy of life is what dies inside a man while he lives."* We are all equipped with a sense in our hearts as to our *Personal Mission*. This is a *"heart sense"*, a *"Calling"*, and it is a picture that is painted of our future. It answers the question of, *Why Were You Born?* When we explore and unearth why we were born, our Personal Mission Statement, and live THAT, we will walk in abundance and fullness, because we are walking in *alignment*.

See, in all of life and nature, *abundance flows from alignment*. We don't expect abundance when the tree does not flow in alignment with the soil and elements of nature. We wouldn't expect a tree to prosper if it was sitting on a bed of hot burning coals. We don't expect abundance when animals do not flow in

---

[33] http://www.wisdomquotes.com/topics/purpose/

alignment with the balance and laws of nature. We wouldn't expect an eagle to prosper if it didn't eat, or if he tried to fly underwater. Why should we expect personal abundance if we live outside of our Personal Mission Statement? Abundance flows from alignment.

This chapter is all about *Exploring & Clarifying Your Mission*. When we do *Explore & Clarify Our Mission*, we flow in alignment with our own nature and the universe. *Abundance always flows from alignment*. The challenge for many of us is narrowing down and *Clarifying* our *Mission*. The philosopher, Soren Kierkegaard expressed the difficulty in this when he said:

> *"What I really lack is to be clear in my mind what I am to do, not what I am to know... the thing is to understand myself, to see what God really wishes me to do... to find the idea for which I can live and die."*

Throughout history, a sense of calling and Personal Mission has been a force that has propelled people to success and amazing heights, again and again, because *abundance flows from alignment*. And the fundamental key in all of this is that this abundance, which flows from alignment, is not only for us, but for the people and the world around us.

There are many definitions for this concept of a **Personal Mission**. My suggestion is that our **Personal Mission** is the place where our sense of calling and destiny collide with our Gifts & Ability, Passion & Personality to fill in the "gaps" around us. **Our Personal Mission** is discovered at the point where our **Sense Of Calling** combines with **Our Gifts & Ability**, and **Our Passions & Personality, to fill in the "Gaps" all around us:**

- Solving Problems	- Answering Questions,
- Meeting Needs	- Providing Solutions,
- Filling Voids	- Lessening Pain,
- Healing Wounds	- Making A Difference!

Mahatma Gandhi famously said, *"The difference between what we are doing and what we're capable of doing would solve most of the world's problems"*. There is a "*Gap*" between what we are currently doing and what we're capable of doing. We know this by feel and we know it by instinct. It is at the convergence of this "Gap" and our *Gifts & Ability*, and our *Passions & Personality, weave together to form our* Personal Mission Statement.

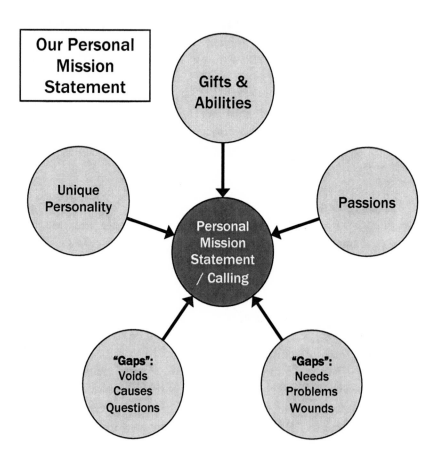

Our Personal Mission *is the place where our sense of calling and destiny collide with our* **Gifts & Ability, Passion, Personality** *to fill in the "Gaps" around us...*

Here is a question for you:

Do you possess a deeply-held belief that you have a calling in life? Do you possess a deep-seated belief that you have a Personal Mission?

When Jim Collins and Jerry Porras studied the *"best of the best"*, in terms of businesses which had stood the test of time and had seen multiple generations of success, here is what they discovered in "Built To Last":

> *"We've learned that purpose – when properly conceived – has a profound effect upon an organization beyond what core values alone can do, and that organizations should put more effort into identifying their purpose."* [34]

See, for success, you must have a Why. When you lose your "Why", you can say, "Good-Bye"! Myles Munroe said, *"Purpose is the master of motivation and the mother of commitment. It is the source of enthusiasm and the womb of perseverance. Purpose gives birth to hope and instils the passion to act."* [35] Maybe the reason that some lack motivation, commitment, enthusiasm, perseverance, hope, passion, and fulfilment is because they lack a clear sense of their purpose, their Mission.

I love the words of W. Clement Stone, who said, *"When you discover your mission, you will feels its demand. It will fill you with enthusiasm and a burning desire to get to work on it."* One reason people fail is simply a lack of sense of Mission. The greatest tragedy is not death, but life without a reason. Without a Mission, life becomes a string of activities with little significance. A life without a Mission moves a lot but gets nowhere, like a rocking horse. Our **Personal Mission** is the place where our sense of calling and destiny collide with our *Gifts & Ability*, and our *Passion & Personality*, to fill in the **"Gaps"** around us.

---

[34] *Built To Last*, Jim Collin and Jerry Porras, HarperCollins Books, 1994, p.xx

[35] Myles Munroe, *In Pursuit Of Purpose* (Shippensburg, PA: Destiny Image Publishers 1992), Introduction

Charles Garfield said, "The mission statement provides the why that inspires every how". In "The Purpose Driven Organization", Perry Pascarella and Mark A. Froham said, "Purpose is not simply a target that an organization chooses to aim for; it is the organization's reason for being" [36]. So, our Personal Mission Statement sums up our reason for being. Ultimately, success means having the courage, the determination, and the will to become the person you believe you were meant to be. The challenge for some is in clarifying this Mission.

Your Personal Mission Statement is that statement which defines why you are here; a brief, broad, bold, motivating statement that describes why you were born and exist. Our Personal Mission *is the place where our sense of calling and destiny collide with our Gifts & Ability,* and our *Passion & Personality, to fill in the "gaps" around us.* Rick Warren said, *"Nothing precedes purpose. The starting point... should be the question, 'Why do we exist?' Until you know what you...exist for, you have no foundation, no motivation, and no direction..."[37]* Fred Smith said, *"Nothing is as necessary for success as the single-minded pursuit of an objective".* When you lose your *"Why",* you can say, *"Good-Bye"!* When we lose the quality of being **MISSION-DRIVEN**, two things happen:

We Plateau – We level off and slow or stop a growth cycle,

We Stagnate – Soon we begin to shrink and decline.

There can be no doubt, when we look at history and at the annals of those who made a difference, that they were captured, captivated, and motivated by a Personal Mission Statement. Abraham Lincoln was driven by a Personal Mission Statement to correct injustice and have a nation of law and order. Martin Luther King Jr. was inspired by a Personal Mission Statement to bring fairness and equality. Nelson Mandela was captured by a Personal

[36] Glenn Van Ekeren, *Speaker's Sourcebook II* (Paramus, NJ: Prentice Hall 1994), 254.
[37] Rick Warren, *The Purpose Driven Church* (Grand Rapids, Mich.: Zondervan Publishing House 1995), 81.

Mission Statement of freedom from oppression and rep
Winston Churchill felt compelled by a Personal
Statement to stand up for his country in the midst of a k
situation. We all need a Personal Mission Statement.

Developing A Personal Mission Statement

The Personal Mission Statement should be a clear and concise statement of your purpose for existence. The **Personal Mission Statement (PMS)** can be very simple, and it can also be a very complex set of ideas. A Personal Mission is *the place where our sense of calling and destiny collide with our Gifts & Ability, Passion & Personality to fill in the "gaps" around us.* The PMS simply sums this up in an unambiguous, clear, and brief way.

As we begin this journey, I love the words of Po Bronson: *"You want a step? Step one: Stop pretending we're all on the same staircase."*[38] I love that! There is a different pathway for all of us! There is no set way to develop a PMS. But, there is a simple process which I will describe here to facilitate you as you seek to develop a PMS. It follows 3 stages:

THE PMS PROCESS:

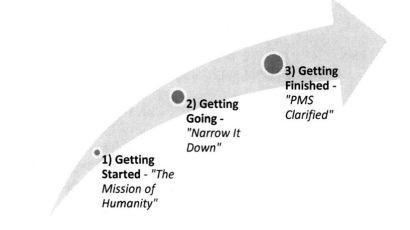

3) Getting Finished - "PMS Clarified"

2) Getting Going - "Narrow It Down"

1) Getting Started - "The Mission of Humanity"

---

[38] Po Bronson, *What Should I Do With My Life?* Random House, Toronto 2002: p.xv

1) Getting Started – "The Mission Of Humanity"

Remember: *Abundance always flows from alignment*. The more closely aligned we are with our specific Mission, the more abundance will flow. And, though we all have a specific Mission, we *all* have a general purpose, which extends to all of us as humanity. Our specific Mission flows from our general purpose as human beings. Here are a few thoughts on our general purpose:

Your Purpose....

☙ **To Know** – Our purpose, and part of why we were put on this planet, is to deeply and fundamentally know *who we are*, to know *who we are not*, and to know *what we are meant to do*. Blaise Pascal said, *"Our achievements of today are but the sum total of our thoughts of yesterday. You are today where the thoughts of yesterday have brought you and you will be tomorrow where the thoughts of today take you"*. Part of this is also to know *the worth and value of other people*, and to treat them like treasure.

☙ **To Flow** – With who and what you are. Living in alignment with yourself is absolutely crucial! Do not try to become someone you are not, because *abundance flows from alignment*. Our purpose is to live and flow in alignment with our passions and personality and gifts and abilities.

☙ **To Grow** – Constant and continual growth in our personal lives, our relationships, and our professional lives is extremely healthy. When we stop growing, we start dying. *Intellectual growth, emotional* growth, *relational* growth, *financial* growth, *social* growth, *professional* growth: these are all crucial keys to a life of purpose and contentment. As long as we are living and breathing, we have the power to keep on growing!

❧ **To Sow** – Our purpose as human beings is to come to a place of abundance and fruitfulness ourselves, and then to sow seeds into the lives of others. I love the quote that, *"We make a living from what we* get, *but a life from what we* give.*"* Buddha described the purpose of our lives as givers like this: *"Thousands of candles can be lit from a single candle, and the life of the candle will not be shortened. Happiness never decreases by being shared."* We were born to light the candles of others, sowing rich seeds into their lives, and as we do, we only add to their happiness while
taking nothing away from our own!

2) Getting Going – "Narrow It Down"

This is basically Brainstorming, which doesn't allow for negative thoughts or energy. The more ideas, the better. Typically, it follows three ground rules:

• No "pre-emptive strikes" on ideas – i.e., letting them all flow

• No negative thoughts

• An abundance of ideas

• The purpose of brainstorming is coming up with ideas in a positive atmosphere.

My Personal Mission

What do I sense God/the Universe has called me to do with my life?_____

_____

_____

What can I see myself doing for the rest of my life?_____

_____

_____

What do I believe in so much that I could give my life to it?

_____

_____

_____

About what could I say, "I'll be miserable if I do not do this..."?

_____

_____

What have others said about my Personal Mission? _____

_____

_____

What do I live for? _____

_____

What would I die for?_____

_____

What puts meaning and value into my life? _____

_____

_____

In what areas could I say, like Martin Luther, "Here I stand. I can't do anything else"? _____

_____

Where do I want to place my limited resources of time, talent and treasure? _____

_____

_____

In what can I become constructively obsessed? _____

_____

_____

What needs, injustices, hurts, and causes trigger an emotional reaction in me? _____

_____

_____

A **Personal Mission** is the place where our sense of calling and destiny collide with our **Gifts & Ability**, and our **Passion & Personality**, to fill in the "**Gaps**" around us. Which "**Gaps**" seem most natural for you to fill?_____

_____

_____

_____

3) Getting Finished – "PMS Clarified"

A **Personal Mission** is the place where our sense of calling and destiny collide with our Gifts & Ability, and our Passion & Personality, to fill in the "gaps" around us. The PMS simply sums this up in an unambiguous, clear, and brief way. Here we hammer out our exact Personal Mission Statement. Your PMS should pass the "T-shirt Test", which is, would it fit onto a t-shirt? **Your PMS should be:**

Crisp – Clear and to the point.

Creative – Fresh. Not old, dated, or stale.

Captivating – Language that inspires and captures the imagination.

Complete – Does the STATEMENT give all the components of your MISSION?

Communicated – Communicate, using every method, your **PMS**. Let others know what is most important to you!

Your Personal Mission Statement:

As we conclude this chapter, the key is **Living Your LIFEFIT**. We need to **live** our **LIFEFIT**. It is healthy to live and flow in a way that is aligned and congruent with our **LIFEFIT**. Live in a way that flows with your Personal Mission Statement. A Personal Mission is *the place where our sense of calling and destiny collide with our Gifts & Ability,* and our *Passion & Personality*, to *fill in the "gaps" around us.* When you look at your PMS, it may seem difficult. At first, any dream seems *impossible*, but as we work it, put some sweat equity and passion into it and move forward, it becomes *improbable*. Eventually, with enough effort and faith and positive energy, we create a momentum where our PMS becomes *inevitable*. As my friend Brent says, *"Everyone who has ever taken a shower has had an idea. It's the person who gets out of the shower, dries off, and does something about it that makes a difference."* So cool! My best advice is this: take a shower! Dream some dreams! Get some ideas! Then, dry off and go to work! Live your PMS!

Getting Where You Need To Go
Chapter 8 – "F" –
Facilitating & Developing Marketable Skills

To *Get Where We Need To Go*, we need to Learn About Our **Passions**, and Investigate Our **Personality**. We also need to Find Out Our **Gifts & Abilities,** and Explore & Clarify Our **Mission.** This comes in the form of a Personal Mission Statement. Next, to *Get Where You Need To Go*, we need to Facilitate & Develop Our **Marketable Skills.** It is wise to consistently deepen our pool of expertise.

There is a huge trend in our information age and information culture towards life-long learning and continuing education. We live in a world speeding towards the future, where the knowledge and skill you had even 5 years ago no longer gets you the results it once did, or the pay cheque. What you knew, and what worked, just a few years ago may no longer work today, and at the very least, may not provide the income, security, and status it once did. A former Prime Minister of the United Kingdom, Harold Wilson, said, *"He who rejects change is the architect of decay. The only human institution which rejects progress is the cemetery."*

There are many ways people are describing our economy today. We are known as a *"knowledge"* economy, a *"skills-based"* economy, an *"information-technology"* economy, and a *"new"* economy. These terms reflect the fact that our economy today is built much more around a knowledge and skill base, and much more around information technology, than ever before. The key to employment security and a steady paycheque is the ability to change and organically evolve; to continually transform and flow with the realities of the marketplace around us. Vincent Van Gogh, the impressionist painter, was a schoolmaster, student priest missionary and art dealer before he became a painter. Before he became President, Abraham Lincoln was a rail splitter, a riverboat operator, a store clerk/owner, a postmaster, a surveyor, a military officer, a lawyer, and finally, a politician. They did what they needed to do so they were employable and working and able to earn with ever changing Marketable Skills. I came across an interesting article that describes some of the challenges we are all facing today:

> *"The New Economy is more dynamic, faster, and entrepreneurial. With dynamism, however, comes risk. Up to a third of all jobs are in flux every year (meaning they have either recently been added to, or will soon be eliminated from, the economy). As new companies spring up and established companies respond to change and competition, fewer workers can look forward to long careers with a single employer. For example, median job tenure for males declined from around six years in the mid-1980s to five years in 2000.*
>
> *Second, it means that the old forms of security workers enjoyed -- bound up as they were in large stable corporations, strong unions, and the welfare state -- have dramatically declined. Employees must now continually reinvent themselves throughout their working lives, even if they remain with the same employer. And the responsibility for getting the education and training an employee needs has shifted from the company to the individual. As a result, skills and adaptability have become the new job security."* [39] (Emphasis mine)

This *"continual reinvention"* of ourselves is the heart of *Facilitating & Developing Marketable Skills*. We need to be far more tethered to the concept that we are continually changing and evolving and *Facilitating & Developing Marketable Skills* than the concept that, *"I am a software programmer or machine operator or receptionist or cell-phone salesperson or accountant or whatever I am."* In other words, our priority must be consistently *Facilitating & Developing Marketable Skills*, rather than settling for our career at the moment or what we were trained to do yesterday. The Bureau of Labor Statistics reports that men and women hold an average of 14 jobs by the time they turn 40 [40].

---

[39] http://www.dlc.org/documents/build_skills2.pdf, p.1
[40] http://jobs.lovetoknow.com/Career_Change_Statistics

Now of course, some of this is simply people finding themselves and what they enjoy, as job longevity tends to lengthen as people age. However, some of this is bound up in the fact that in our new economy, constant change means we need to constantly change to be able to earn. LifeTwo, a leading career counselling organization, reports that their prior estimate of three careers in a lifetime is now in the process of increasing to as many as seven [41]. I have often heard from Career Coaches that people will change careers on average six to eight times within their lifetime.

The truth is we need to be far more tethered to the concept that we are continually changing and evolving and *Facilitating & Developing Marketable Skills*, than to the concept of being tied to one career or skill set or level of education. We need to embrace the mindset of change and constant growth. We need to continually *Facilitate & Develop* an abundance of *Marketable Skills*. The need for continual education and the constant learning of learn new skills has never been greater. Truthfully, our only income security is our ability to change, grow, and develop more *Marketable Skills*. At a conference between the United States and the European Union on The Labor Market in the 21st Century, Thomas B. Moorhead, then Deputy Under Secretary for International Labor Affairs, U.S. Department of Labor, made some important comments about changes and shifts in our economy today. Though he made them specific to the United States, it is clear that these comments would apply globally within their specific contexts:

> "...*acquiring skills pays off, and there is a growing demand for skills:*
> - *In the United States, the unemployment rate for a high school dropout is four times the rate for a college graduate.*
> - *The earnings gap between high school and college graduates has ballooned to 70 percent.*
> - *Over the next 10 years, 4 out of every 10 new jobs will require a postsecondary vocational or academic*

---

[41] http://jobs.lovetoknow.com/Career_Change_Statistics

| *degree.* " [42]

We need to be far more tethered to the concept that we are continually evolving and *Facilitating & Developing Marketable Skills,* rather than to the concept of being attached to one career or skill set or level of education.

One of the great things about being Canadian is the diversity of our country. We have massive forests, an abundance of fresh water, fertile and vast tracts of farmland, mountain ranges for thousands of kilometres, access to three different oceans, and every type land and geology one could imagine. We have perhaps the largest raw resource base in the world, with ready access to pulp and paper, minerals, agriculture, fisheries, oil and natural gas. We have the second largest verified oil reserves in the world.

This has led to an economy with a huge reliance on natural resources, and on the manufacturing and heavy industry that accompany them. Of course, this has had a major impact on our people, our industry, and on how people make a living. I grew up in Ontario, our manufacturing heartland, where many spent their whole lives working in manufacturing plants and heavy industry. When recession hit, those with the fewest *Marketable Skills* were hurt the most as the economy shifted rapidly. Many were not in a position to respond and react accordingly. This trend is repeated often in rural or resource-based regional economies. In centres likes these, often huge segments of the economy are focused on fishing, mining, pulp and paper, and small manufacturing. There are small communities where the only skills people learn since youth are fishing or forestry or mining. When the fish or the trees or the minerals run out, they may have no other *Marketable Skills.* We all need to constantly explore, hone and develop not just our *Skills* but our *Marketable Skills.* It is not the strongest of the species that survive, nor the most intelligent, but the ones most responsive to change. Once again, we need to be far more tethered to the concept that we are continually evolving and *Facilitating & Developing Marketable Skills*, rather than to the concept of being attached to one career or skill set or level of education.

---

[42] http://www.dol.gov/ilab/media/reports/otla/labormarkskills/labormarkskills.htm

There is an ancient Hebrew Proverb that I love. It is simple and yet elegantly effective: *"If the ax is dull, and one does not sharpen the edge, then he must use more strength; but wisdom brings success"*. Years ago, like most young men, I thought I was invincible and quite possibly the strongest man in the world. There was a stack of firewood that needed to be cut to the proper size for use in the fireplace. So I grabbed the old axe and started chopping. It was hard. Sweat was dripping off my forehead, yet I was making very little progress. I had the good sense to check the blade on the axe and realized how dull the blade was. It wasn't that the blade was old; simply that it was dull. I grabbed the other axe with the sharp blade and made short work of the wood.

In other words, if I am chopping wood with my axe, the age of the blade is not the issue so much as its sharpness. If my blade is sharp, the work is not nearly as difficult as if my blade is dull. Perhaps it was from this ancient Hebrew Proverb that Abraham Lincoln found the thought for his famous quote: *"Give me six hours to chop down a tree and I will spend the first four sharpening the axe"*. In other words, *effectiveness* is not about working *hard*, but working *smart*. This is *Facilitating & Developing Marketable Skills.*

What Is The Difference Between A Skill And A Marketable Skill? The Key Question Is This: Are They Marketable? In other words, Will People <u>Pay</u> For Them?

We need to continually Develop new Marketable Skills so that we can work *smarter* as opposed to *harder*. Let's constantly ask ourselves how we can improve our *Marketable Skills* so that our personal, financial and career ceilings are broken. Many are waiting to win the lottery or to have money pushed off a cloud into their lap. A more effective approach is to develop *Marketable Skills*. The more *Marketable Skills* we have, the greater our potential. *Every time we develop a new Marketable Skill, we break through another financial ceiling.* With each new *Marketable Skill* comes a possible new stream of income, opportunity for promotion, and possibility for greater success.

Once again, *Marketable Skills* = What People Will Pay You To Do. When we evaluate ourselves in terms of our *Marketable Skills*, we need to be tough on ourselves. When we think we have a *Marketable Skill*, we have to ask a simple question: *Will people pay me to do this?* If you are not sure, ask a few people who have been successful in business for more than 5 years. They will tell you for sure if your *Skill* is just a *Skill*, or if it is a *Marketable Skill*.

- The More Marketable Skills You Have, The More *Options* You Have…

- The More Marketable Skills You Have, The More *Useful* You Are…

- The More Marketable Skills You Have, The More *Income* Streams You Have…

- Marketable Skills *Pay* The Bills…

- Marketable Skills Can Be Your Income, Or An Income Supplement…

Marketable Skills

Constantly Change – What was *Marketable* (i.e. people pay you for it) just a few years ago is not necessarily *Marketable* today. There is not a huge need for service techs for VHS video tape players. And what was *Marketable* in a particular location today is not necessarily *Marketable* in that same location tomorrow. In other words, a person with a *Marketable Skill* of carpentry generally needs to be mobile and go where the work is if she wants steady income. *Marketable Skills* are constantly changing. Sometimes we fight change. When we do, we should remember the words of W. Edwards Deming: *"It is not necessary to change.*

Survival is not mandatory". Survival and success are always just optional.

Create Options – *Marketable Skills*, more than anything else, simply give us options. As the economy changes around us, conditions change, governments change and business changes. The more *Marketable Skills* we have, the more opportunity we have.

Cost You – *Marketable Skills* are not free. Nothing that adds true value in life is free. Get into the mindset of being willing to pay for the things that add value to you. Getting Certified as a Life Coach or Life Skills Instructor or Microsoft Professional or Graphic Designer or First Aid Instructor or Lab Technician or Data Processor or Server Technician or Adult Learning Facilitator or ESL Instructor or Management Professional, or whatever, will cost you. But it is worth it! Pay the price, by focusing on the prize! *Facilitating & Developing Marketable Skills* often costs the following:

Time –
It takes time to learn, time to grow, time to evolve.

Money –
It costs money to invest in your greatest resource: **YOU!**

Focus –
It takes focus to study and continually learn and evolve.

Hard Work –
Growth and education is hard work. It takes discipline.

Stick-ability –
When we want to quit, we gotta keep on keepin' on!

What Marketable Skills Should You Develop?

One of the most exciting things about our digital age is the absolute abundance of options when it comes to *Facilitating & Developing Marketable Skills.* People used to be limited to the community college in their town or city, or hope that the local university offered night classes. Today, so long as you have access to a computer and Internet connection, you can develop *Marketable Skills* wherever you are, in almost whatever area you choose. There are so many options today, and often that becomes a hindrance in and of itself. Too many options can make any decision difficult. Here is some guidance for making that choice:

Know Your Market – Take time to research your local market and see where the needs are. Every market generally has gaps in terms of skilled workers and qualified people in certain areas. Make an appointment with a career counsellor or do some research on your local government's website to see where the identifiable needs are. Better yet, check your local employment classifieds or websites such as Workopolis or Monster to see what gaps employers are identifying. Knowing your market and its ever-changing needs is essential.

Know Your Business Network – Part of researching your local market is also tapping into and knowing what your own business network is saying. We all have a personal business network, from our LinkedIn and Facebook and Twitter account, to our local hairdresser, to our dentist and the person working at the grocery checkout or at a 7-11, to people at associations and organizations we are a part of, to people we come into contact with in our day job, to our server at a local restaurant, and on and on. Each person we come into contact with from a business perspective has their finger on the pulse of their piece of the local market. Find out what they are saying. Pick their brains. Learn from them. You may find a lot more information than you imagined.

Know Your Options – Take time to research local schools, community colleges, career training centres, colleges and universities, and various training courses and certification programs. See what is offered in terms of online learning that has credibility and acceptance in the broader market. Lastly, do research around funding options and see if there are scholarships or loan programs available to help you financially as you pursue more *Marketable Skills*.

Know Your Competition – Take time to find out what the learning trends are in terms of *Marketable Skills*. Find out current enrolments at local agencies and schools doing training, and see which way the wind is blowing from a market perspective. Have a look at where there is an over-saturation of training and avoid those areas. Ask what *Marketable Skills* others are training for and learn from that.

Know Yourself – To be really effective in any area of life or *Marketable Skills*, we need to know ourselves. Confucius said, *"If you choose a job you like, you will never have to work a day in your life"*. We have taken a detailed look at the following:

- Your *Passions*   - Your *Gifts & Abilities*
- Your *Personality*   - Your *Personal Mission*

Add to the above the following, when it comes to *Marketable Skills:*

- Your Previous Careers   - Your Connections
- Your Life Experiences   - Your Intuition About Yourself
- Your Opportunities, i.e. where people are opening doors for you in terms of training.

The more honest you are in assessing these qualities, the more you will be able to truly say you know yourself.

Know What Those Close To You Are Saying – Lastly, take a small survey of the people closest to you, those who see your potential and believe in you, and ask what they think and feel about what *Marketable Skills* you should develop. Their answers may pleasantly surprise you!

How Can We Increase Our Marketable Skills?

Through A Lifelong Learning Mindset – Always have the mind of a student and a learner. Have the humility to be a person who is constantly exploring, discovering and developing. The mindset of a student keeps the brain sharp, and the resume packed. When the student is ready, teachers appear. The learning journey should never end.

Through Training & Skill Development – When is the last time you took a course, earned a degree, or gained a new certification? When is the last time you sat in a classroom or learning environment and developed a new skill-set, gained a better way of operation, or learned new concepts? Begin the practice of setting aside 2-5% of your annual income to training, skill development, and learning. You will only be paying yourself!

Through Experience – Don't shy away from things you consider below you if they build valuable experience. People pay more for *Marketable Skills* you have experience in, than those you do not. Businesses pay significant dollars for experience, because experience often saves time and money in the end.

Through Developing People Skills – Many with above average *Marketable Skills* make below average income, simply because they lack people skills. The soft skills of mutual respect, consideration, teamwork, emotional intelligence, social intelligence, humility, selflessness, gentleness, active listening, kindness, diligence and fair play go a long way! Teddy Roosevelt was known to say, *"The single most important ingredient to the formula of success is knowing how to get along with people!"*

Now, the reality is that no matter what *Marketable Skills* one develops, some with above average *Marketable Skills* earn below average incomes. The reason is simple: They are lacking other *Key Skills*. We need to add to our *Marketable Skills* several other *Key Skills:*

5 Keys Skills That Will increase Your Earnings

Foundational Skills – It may sound harsh, but some people are simply lazy. All their skills and talents go to waste. No matter how many *Marketable Skills* we have, without the *Foundational Skills* of hard work, diligence, follow-through, and stick-ability, we will not have long-lasting and durable success. Nothing works until you do! All the so called *"secrets of success"* do not work until we do! Thomas Jefferson nailed it when he said: *"I'm a great believer in luck, and I find the harder I work the more I have of it."*

Social Skills – Social skills can broadly be defined as the ability to get along with people and, in time, develop an effective network. One might use the moniker **"S.W.A.G."** here: *"Socializing With A Goal"*. I learned a long time ago in leadership that to be effective, we need to be both respected and liked. If you are liked, but not necessarily respected, it is camaraderie. If you are respected but not liked, it is simply fear. We need both to be effective.

Communication Skills – Learning the two elements of effective communication are crucial: *Listening* well, and *Speaking* well. A person who is both a *perceptive listener*, and *persuasive speaker*, often succeeds at whatever they do and win a lot of fans along the way!

Digital/Computer Skills – We don't all need to become software developers, but understanding the basics of computers and how to navigate them, word processing, spreadsheets, email, time management software, and Internet access are crucial for success in any field today. The essentials might only be Microsoft Office or iWork, and the Internet Browser of your choice.

Problem-Solving Skills – People pay for those who solve problems, as opposed to those who either create them, or those who just can't solve them and simply drop them onto someone else's desk. Business owners, managers, and Executives pay significant dollars for people who are able to solve problems, see solutions, identify opportunities, and re-frame difficulties. Ask yourself if you simply identify problems, or if you have developed the art of also offering solutions and alternatives.

As we conclude this chapter, the key is **Living Your LIFEFIT**. We need to live our **LIFEFIT.** It is healthy to live in a way that is aligned and congruent with our **LIFEFIT**. Live in a way that flows with your *Passions, Personality, Gifts & Abilities*, and your *Personal Mission*. Then, top them all off with *Facilitating & Developing Marketable Skills*.

The only constant is change. So, we need to be far more tethered to the concept that we are continually evolving and *Facilitating & Developing Marketable Skills*, than to the concept of being tied to one career or skill set or level of education. We need to take the mindset of change and constant growth. We need to continually *Facilitate & Develop* an abundance of *Marketable Skills*, because every *Marketable Skill* opens up another income stream and breaks through another ceiling. Marketable Skills create opportunity, break personal barriers, careers barriers, and drive income.

Willa A. Foster said: *"Quality is never an accident; it is always the result of high intention, sincere effort, intelligent direction and skilful execution; it represents the wise choice of many alternatives."* I love that! Quality is never an accident. Look at it like this:

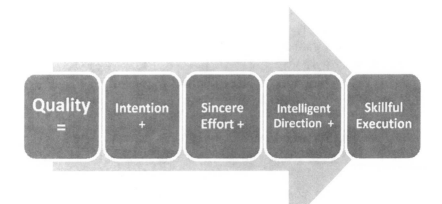

Lastly, *take responsibility.* It is not your family's responsibility, or society's responsibility, or the government's responsibility to get you the *Marketable Skills* you need. It is your responsibility, and yours alone. Maturing is moving towards personal responsibility. Take responsibility, and continually *Facilitate & Develop Marketable Skills!*

Getting Where You Need To Go
Chapter 9 – "*I*" –
Include Networking & Relationships

It was a day like any other. I went into work at the high-volume big-box senior management position I had at the time, trying to work hard, and to work smart. As I left my office and went into the Staff Lounge, I saw something that I had seen countless times before. I had witnessed the same scene in malls, stores, coffee shops, restaurants, sidewalks, bus stops, and of course, in that same Staff Lounge, time after time. It was a simple picture. A young lady, sitting on chair, alternating between talking on her smart phone, sending and receiving text messages, and downloading her latest emails. Of course, I had observed this exact picture hundreds of times before, but this time it just hit me. It had impact, and it had resonance.

Seeing someone using the cell phone is not uncommon. Everywhere you go, on public transit, and in malls, restaurants, and shops, people are texting away, talking away, and connecting with someone on the other end of their mobile phone. I was in Africa in 2005, and what struck me, more than almost anything else, was that it seemed like everyone had a "pay as you go" mobile phone. It surprised me. The use of mobile phones and smart phones has exploded in the last 30-35 years. The first hand held phone was demonstrated by Martin Cooper of Motorola in 1973, using a handset weighing in at two kilos. In 1990, 12.4 million people worldwide had cellular subscriptions. By the end of 2009, only 20 years later, the number of mobile cellular subscriptions worldwide reached 4.6 billion, 300 times the 1990 number, penetrating the developing economies and reaching the both the top and bottom of the economic pyramid [43]. Wow! 4.6 billion cell phones on the planet, almost one for every person!

Back in the Staff Lounge, what hit me was not so much the cell phone use, because this is so very common, but the incredibly desperate cry inside of each one of us for connection. This

---

[43] http://en.wikipedia.org/wiki/Mobile_phone

incredibly common occurrence of a person on a phone was re-framed for me in the context of people's longing and cry for connection, for intimacy, for community, and for true partnership. There is a longing implanted in each one of us to care and be cared for, to love and be loved, and to connect with others and be connected to them. This can be seen right from birth to death, from the cradle to the grave; from the cry of an infant longing to be held to the dying gasps of a man or woman wanting someone to hold their hand during their passage from this earth. Maurice Wagner said: *"At the heart of personality is the need to feel a sense of being lovable without having to qualify for that acceptance."*

We all know this to be true. We know so deeply that we don't need the confirmation of scientific studies or validation from the psychological community. We just know it. We feel it. We live it. Even pre-mature babies feel this need and respond when it is met. Preemies massaged 3 times a day, for as few as five days, at the University of Miami's Touch Research Institute are more alert, sleep better, and gain weight faster. The Touch Research Institute has conducted more than 100 studies on the positive effects of massage therapy on many functions and medical conditions in many different age groups. Among the significant research findings are enhanced growth (e.g. in preterm infants), diminished pain (e.g. fibromyalgia), decreased autoimmune problems (e.g. increased pulmonary function in asthma and decreased glucose levels in diabetes), enhanced immune function (e.g. increased natural killer cells in HIV and cancer), and enhanced alertness and performance (e.g. EEG pattern of alertness and better performance on math computations). Many of these effects appear to be mediated by decreased stress hormones.[44] Several years ago, the U.C.L.A. did research that showed the average person needs 8-10 meaningful touches a day to be emotionally and mentally healthy.

Often what we don't realize is the huge cost of not having the need for connection, intimacy, community, and for true partnership met in our lives. When this need is met, we are alive and filled with joy, peace and fulfilment. When it is not met... our desperate cry for relationship can lead to desperate deeds.

---

[44] http://www6.miami.edu/touch-research/Research.html

Desperate cries often lead to desperate deeds. When we feel a hole, we try to fill it. When we sense a need, we try to meet it. Sometimes our choice of what to fill the need with isn't the best. At times our choice of how we seek to meet the need isn't the best choice or the healthiest choice.

In terms of *Getting Where We Need To Go*, the concepts of connection, intimacy, community, and true partnership are *crucial*. We cannot *Get Where We Need To Go alone*.

To *Get Where We Need To Go*, we need to Learn About Our **Passions**, and Investigate Our **Personality**. We also need to Find Out Our **Gifts & Abilities**, and Explore & Clarify Our **Mission**. We need to Facilitate & Develop Our **Marketable Skills**. It is wise to consistently deepen our pool of expertise. Next, to *Get Where We Need To Go*, we need to **Include Networking & Relationships**. We cannot Get Where We Need To Go alone.

To *Get Where You Need To Go*, you need to ask: *"Who Am I Going With?"* You will never *Get Where You Need To Go* alone. The only thing better than doing something great on your own, is doing something great together, with the help and support of others! We all need to be able to stand on the shoulders of others to *Get Where We Need To Go*. Relationships are a crucial key in unlocking your destiny.

There is an ancient Hebrew sacred passage that speaks to the power of *Networking & Relationships*. Though it was written more than 3000 years ago, it is worth a look today. It is in the book of Ecclesiastes 4:9-12:

> *"9Two people can accomplish more than twice as much as one; they get a better return for their labor. 10If one person falls, the other can reach out and help. But people who are alone when they fall are in real trouble. 11And on a cold night, two under the same blanket can gain warmth from each other. But how can one be warm alone? 12A person standing alone can be attacked and defeated, but two can stand back-to-back and conquer. Three are even better, for a triple-braided cord is not easily broken."*

This exposes some deep truths regarding *Networking & Relationships*, and why they are so crucial as we pursue *Getting Where We Need To Go*.

- *Networking & Relationships Exponentially Increase Our Potential.* The passage says, *"Two people can accomplish more than twice as much as one..."* As we pursue *Getting Where We Need To Go*, there is a lot a person can accomplish on their own. However, when we *Network, Partner, & Build Relationships*, there is almost nothing we cannot do. Winston Churchill, when faced with some pretty enormous odds, said, *"If we are together nothing is impossible. If we are divided all will fail."*

- *Networking & Relationships Increase The Return On Our Efforts* – *"Two people... get a better return for their labor."* This better return comes out in greater results, and greater fulfillment. It is more satisfying to achieve with others than it is to achieve alone.

- *Networking & Relationships Are An Incredible Safety Valve* – The passage says, "If one person falls, the other can reach out and help. But people who are alone when they fall are in real trouble." We all stumble, make mistakes, and fall from time to time. It is a reality and we need to accept it. However, getting up from a tumble is a lot easier when we have taken the time to **Network, Partner, & Build Relationships**, because chances are, there will be someone available to pick us up. It is frightening to fall and have no one to help pick you up.

- *Networking & Relationships Keeps The Passion Alive* – *"...But how can one be warm alone?"* It is tough to keep the Passion alive alone. Albert Schweitzer said, *"In everyone's life, at some time, our inner fire goes out. It is then burst into flame by an encounter with another human being. We should all be thankful for those people who rekindle the inner spirit."* When we *Network, Partner, & Build Relationships,* the Passions inherently in us stay hot.

- *Networking & Relationships Provide Strength & Support In Time Of Need* – The passage says, *"A person standing alone can be attacked and defeated, but two can stand back-to-back and conquer. Three are even better, for a triple-braided cord is not easily broken.* " In 1967, The Beatles wrote and recorded the song, "With A Little Help From My Friends". It contains two memorable lines that make a nice jingle but also make a serious point:

"Oh I get by with a little help from my friends, Mmm, gonna try with a little help from my friends. "

So simple but so true. We can endure and withstand so much more when we are surrounded and supported with a little help from our friends!

Personally, I believe in the guidance of destiny and fate. I also believe that destiny and fate are what you make them. However, I believe that if we are looking for it, we will be led into certain *relationships* at certain *times* with certain *people* to do certain *tasks*, for certain *seasons*. This will be our place of blessing and abundance at that moment. Time and history are full of examples of timely partnerships which produced incredible results. As a matter of fact, *Networking, Partnering, & Building Relationships* with the right people is crucial in tapping into *Getting Where You Need To Go*. Often, people's inability to cultivate friends and nurture networks hinders them from *Getting Where They Need To Go*. We produce far more when we are *Networked, Partnered, & Building Relationships* than we do alone.

Some examples of this include Bill and Hillary Clinton, Orville and Wilbur Wright, and the Warner Brothers. Others include Bill Hewlett and Dave Packard (HP), along with Steve Jobs and Steve Wozniak (Apple Computers).

One of the greatest and most stunningly successful partnerships is that of Larry Page and Sergey Brin, which is the Google story. Page and Brin met working on their doctorates in computer science at Stanford University in 1995. Together, they created a proprietary algorithm for a search engine, with the goal of organizing the vast amount of information available on the Internet. Initially called BackRub, the software catalogued search results according to the popularity of pages. Fairly quickly it became apparent that in most cases the most popular results were also the most useful. Presto, another game changer was born.

In 1998, the pair dropped out of Stanford, changed their startup's name to Google, set up shop in a friend's garage, and raised about $1 million in capital from friends, family, and other investors. Initially, Google received 10,000 queries a day (today that number is estimated at 2 billion) and in 1999 the pair received $25 million in venture-capital funding. Five years later Google went public, opening at $85 a share. Google is now the world's Number 1 Internet search engine. In 2009 the company earned $16.5 billion in sales — most of which was generated through ad sales. [45]

See, we need to be careful to develop the fine art of *Networking, Partnering, & Building Relationships*. Often, people's inability to cultivate friends and nurture networks hinders them from *Getting Where They Need To Go!* We produce far more when we are *Networked, Partnered, & Building Relationships* than we do alone. Let's take a look at *8 Keys* to this art and how we can cultivate it in our lives so we can *Get Where We Need To Go*.

The Art Of Networking, Partnering, & Relationships:

- **Aim To Connect** – We need to significantly "up" our level of consciousness when it comes to Networking, Partnering, & Building Relationships. Many of us are too self-absorbed, relationally reserved, or shy, and feel we have nothing to offer. My best advice is to change this right away. You need people, and people need you. You need relationships, and relationships need you. So, turn every event you attend into an opportunity to network. Utilize Facebook, Twitter, and other social media as an opportunity to not only stay in touch with friends, but also build a network which can assist you in the realm of *Getting Where You Need To Go*. Have a mindset that aims to connect and add one quality relationship per month. Always remember, it's not what you know, but who you know.

---

[45] http://images.businessweek.com/ss/08/11/1121_famous_partnerships/

Mike Davidson said: *"It's all about people. It's about networking and being nice to people and not burning any bridges."* [46]

◐ **Aim To Contribute** – As you are aiming to connect, aim also to contribute. Have a mindset that humbly recognizes you only win when you help others win. Help others *Get Where They Need To Go* BEFORE you expect them to help you *Get Where You Need To Go*. Selflessness is absolutely crucial! I don't agree with the method, but the story of Zoran Bulatovic, a Serbian trade official, is a lesson in selflessness. He cut off the little finger of his left hand with a hacksaw and ate it, in protest over wages that in some cases had not been paid in years. He said: *"We, the workers, have nothing to eat. We had to seek some sort of alternative food. I gave them an example. It hurt like hell"* [47]. We don't need to go that far, but we should always aim to contribute to others in significant and thoughtful ways as we *Network & Build Relationships*.

◐ **Aim To Celebrate** – Aim to celebrate, honour and encourage the **LIFEFIT** of others. Find a place in yourself where your heart and mindset is focused on the beauty and uniqueness of those around you. You may be the only one calling out and celebrating their **LIFEFIT**.

◐ **Aim To Care** – There are few replacements for authentic and genuine care. When you really care about another human being, and show it by listening, affirming, and kindness, you not only meet a fundamental need within them, you also unleash a significant desire in them to care for and benefit you. Ralph Waldo Emerson famously said, *"It is one of the most beautiful compensations in life that no man can sincerely try to help another without helping himself"*. So true! Mother

---

[46] http://www.finestquotes.com/select_quote-category-Networking-page-0.htm
[47] http://news.sky.com/skynews/Home/World-News/Serbian-Union-Official-Chops-Off-Finger-And-Eats-It-In-A-Wages-Protest/Article/

Theresa said, *"Kind words can be short and easy to speak, but their echoes are endless"*.

- **Aim To Communicate** – Communication is to a relationship what oxygen is to the lungs, and what blood is to the body. Without effective and thoughtful communication, any relationship can quickly deteriorate into assumption, suspicion and fear. With communication, problems can be solved, needs can be met, and synergies can be realized. Communication always includes effective listening *first*, and *then* effective speaking. It is an art form we should learn well as we seek to *Network, Partner, & Build Relationships.*

- **Aim To Commit** – Don't be afraid to commit when it comes to *Networking, Partnering, & Building Relationships.* Don't commit too soon, but when you find people who can help *Get You Where You Need To Go*, people who you can also help and assist, commit to them. This can be as simple as a monthly coffee chat or weekly email, or a quarterly dinner. It can be a mutual commitment to mentor and support one another. But however it manifests, the principle is this: When we commit to something, anything, we give it the opportunity to grow and flourish within our lives.

- **Aim To Clarify** – Once you have made a commitment to a certain Partnership or Relationship, a crucial next step is to address issues of expectations. Clarify what the relationship should look like and consist of. Give it room to breathe and to grow by clarifying issues such as how much time you will spend together, the type of commitment you will have, and especially the business side of your relationship, if there is one. When we have expectations that are unspoken, unrealistic, and thus unmet, it leads to conflict and hurt feelings. Elliott Larson said, *"Anger always comes from frustrated expectations"*.

- **Aim To Collaborate** – There is nothing that can draw you closer together and add value in a particular partnership or relationship than to collaborate and work together on a concept, project, task, dream, or joint venture. It is amazing what collaboration and the input of others will do to a dream or idea. Oliver Wendell Holmes rightly said, *"Many ideas grow better when transplanted into another mind than the one where they sprang up"*. That's so true. I come up with a *thought*, and share it with you, and you add some value to it, and it becomes a *concept*. You share it with another, who also adds value, and now it becomes a *dream*. It is shared with another who gives insight and feedback, and the dream becomes a *plan*. Isaac Newton was realistically humble when he said, *"If I have seen further it is by standing on the shoulders of giants"*.

Lastly, here is a little advice when it comes to *Networking, Partnering, & Relationships*. Look at the *Relationships* you now have, and ask yourself:

a) **Should I Grow It?** Some relationships you currently have with others, you need to grow and expand to be able to *Get Where You Need To Go.* You need some of what they have working in their lives to be able to experience the results they experience!

b) **Should I Sow Into It?** Some relationships with others you need to sow into because you are meant to be a blessing, a support, a coach, and a guide to them. Once again, it's not all about you. When you sow quality mentoring, you reap quality mentoring! When you help someone else *Get Where They Need To Go*, good karma is released to help you *Get Where You Need To Go!*

c) **Should I Throw It?** Some relationships actually hurt you and thus hinder you from *Getting Where You Need To Go.* Unhealthy relationships can even feel good at the time, but add no value to us in the end. Why continue with a relationship that is not for your benefit if it puts at risk your own destiny and future? My best advice is simple: Chuck em!

d) **Should I Leave It?** Some relationships with others neither harm nor help you. So, simply leave those relationships where they are at. A relationship that looks like it adds a neutral value to you now may add a positive value in the future. The more relationships you have, the more possible sources of help, support and abundance you have!

As we conclude this chapter, the key is Living Your **LIFEFIT**. We need to **live** our **LIFEFIT**. It is healthy to live aligned and congruent with our **LIFEFIT**. Live in a way that flows with your *Passions, Personality, Gifts & Abilities*, and *Personal Mission*. Top them all off with *Facilitating & Developing Marketable Skills*. Next, we need to *Include Networking & Relationships*. We cannot *Get Where We Need To Go* alone. *To Get Where You Need To Go*, you need to ask: *"Who Am I Going With?"* Relationships are a crucial key in unlocking your destiny. George Bernard Shaw said, *"If you have an apple and I have an apple and we exchange these apples then you and I will still each have one apple. But if you have an idea and I have an idea and we exchange these ideas, then each of us will have two ideas"*. This is the power of Networking, Partnering, & Building Relationships. Let's commit and learn the fine art of *Networking, Partnering, & Building Relationships!*

Getting Where You Need To Go
Chapter 10 – *"T"* –
Taking Opportunities As They Arise

There is an ancient story told of a ruthless emperor who once held an extremely lavish celebration. Everybody who was anybody in the empire was invited to this party. It was definitely the *place to be*. All the heads of the provinces and important government officials were invited. Unlike most parties, which may last for a few solid hours, this party lasted for six months. It was meant to be a demonstration of the wealth, glamour, and glory of the empire. When the 6-month celebration concluded, the emperor held a banquet for 7 days to top it all off. He invited everyone from the capital city of the empire, from the least to the greatest, to this banquet. Say what you like, but the guy knew how to party!

At the end of this 7-day banquet, the emperor, having consumed a steady stream of alcohol for the last 6 months, made a request. His wife, the queen, an extremely beautiful woman, was commanded to parade before the emperor and all the assembled guests at the party as the evening's entertainment. He wanted to show off her beauty before the crowd and dance around as some sort of spectacle. She rightfully refused this request and denied the emperor his drunken-fuelled pleasure.

The emperor flew into a rage. He declared that she was no longer his queen. And no longer his wife. He ordered a competition to find the most beautiful woman in the empire. Suitable candidates were tracked down and taken to the capital. There they underwent 12 months of preparation, before the day when the emperor would select his favourite. When that day came he made his choice. He picked a young lady named Esther. They married, and Esther became the new queen.

Some time later, there was more drama in the empire – this time because of the Prime Minister. He was even more ruthless and self-absorbed than the emperor. The Prime Minister wanted to do some ethnic cleansing. This was before the days of the United Nations or Human Rights Commissions. As long as the emperor signed the decree, an ethnic group could be abused, mistreated, and even wiped off the map. He made his case to the emperor, and the emperor signed the decree.

What no one realized was that the new queen was a member of this particular ethnic group. It is not known if she tried to cover that fact up, or if the topic simply never came up, but take a moment with me and look at the situation. The Prime Minister wants to do some ethnic cleansing and picks the ethnic group of the new queen. No one knows she belongs to that ethnic group, and this unknown factor creates an unforeseen dynamic. Talk about compounding an evil choice (*ethnic cleansing*) with a stupid choice (*ethnic cleansing the race of the new queen*).

This was a moment of *opportunity* disguised as a *crisis* in which Esther needed to take a *risk*. The new queen could either hide her identity and watch her people experience terrible pain, or she could share her identity, plead with the king, and try to save her race. At this moment of opportunity, like many of us, she hesitated. She weighed the options and looked at *the cost of the opportunity*, which could involve risking her own life and at the very least risking her position as the queen. She measured it against the *opportunity cost* of *not* acting, namely, the possible destruction of her race. As she was pondering this, a close family member came to see her and said the words which sealed the deal in the book of Esther 4:14: *"...you have come to royal position for such a time as this...".* This was a moment of *opportunity* where a young lady had been properly positioned in the middle of a *crisis*, at the right moment and the right place at the right time, and needed to *seize* it.

To *Get Where We Need To Go*, we need to Learn About Our **Passions**, and Investigate Our **Personality**. We also need to Find Out Our *Gifts & Abilities*, and Explore & Clarify Our **Mission**. We need to Facilitate & Develop Our **Marketable Skills**. We definitely need to Include **Networking & Relationships**. We cannot *Get Where We Need To Go* alone. Relationships are a crucial key in unlocking your destiny.

Lastly, we need to cultivate the precise skill and craft of **Taking Opportunities As They Arise**. I cannot overstate the case that if we Learn About Our **Passions**, Investigate Our **Personality**,

Find Out Our *Gifts & Abilities*, Explore & Clarify Our *Mission*, Facilitate & Develop Our *Marketable Skills*, and Include *Networking & Relationships*, but do not hone the art of *Taking Opportunities As They Arise,* it could all be wasted.

We need to learn to *Take Opportunities As They Arise*; to learn to *"seize the moment"*. Many are looking so hard for the *perfect* Opportunity that they miss the *right* Opportunity! This is the *paralysis of analysis*. At times, we find ourselves minimizing Opportunities that come along, because they appear too small or not exactly what we are looking for, when they could very well lead us exactly *Where We Need To Go*. Hugh Allen said it like this: *"Jumping at several small opportunities may get us there more quickly than waiting for one big one to come along"*.

On the other hand, we certainly don't want to just jump at anything and everything that comes along. If I took advantage of every Opportunity that came my way, I would be broke, discouraged, and totally out of gas. So, we need to cultivate the fine art of *Taking Opportunities As They Arise*.

"Carpe Diem" is usually translated from the Latin as *"seize the day"*, or sometimes as *"enjoy the day, pluck the day when it is ripe"*. The original source for the Latin phrase is Horace in *Odes Book I*:

> "Dum loquimur, fugerit invida aetas:
> carpe diem, quam minimum credula postero"

which translates as:

> "While we're talking, envious time is fleeing:
> seize the day, put no trust in the future"

Lord Byron was the first to integrate it into English in his 1817 *'Letters'*, which was published in 1830 by T. Moore: *"I never anticipate - carpe diem - the past at least is one's own, which is one reason for making sure of the present."* [48]

---

[48] http://www.phrases.org.uk/meanings/carpe-diem.html

124

I love that! *"Carpe Diem"*... *"seize the day"*... *"enjoy the day, pluck the day when it is ripe"*. Seize the day, grab hold of the occasion as it presents itself, and make the most of the moment! Enjoy the day and show it by *plucking the day when it is ripe!* There is a Chinese Proverb that simply says something like: *"Enjoy yourself. It's later than you think"*. *Take Opportunities As They Arise!*

The truth is we either seize the moment or we are seized by the moments & events around us. much of life, and building success in life, is about learning not to be controlled by events, but about influencing and seizing events yourself. *Take Opportunities As They Arise!*

Years ago, an energetic young man began as a clerk in a hardware store. Like many old-time hardware stores, the inventory included thousands of dollars worth of items that were obsolete or seldom called for by customers. The young man was smart enough to know that no thriving business could carry all that inventory and still show a healthy profit. He proposed a sale to get rid of the stuff. The owner was reluctant but finally agreed to let him set up a table in the middle of the store and try to sell off a few of the oldest items. Every product was priced at ten cents. The sale was a success and the young fellow got permission to run a second sale. It went over just as well as the first. This gave the young clerk an idea. Why not open a store that would sell only nickel and dime items? He could run the store and his boss could supply the capital.

The young man's boss was not enthusiastic. *"The plan will never work"*, he said, *"because you can't find enough items to sell at a nickel and a dime"*. The young man was disappointed but eventually went ahead on his own and made a fortune out of the idea. His name was F.W. Woolworth.

Years later his old boss lamented, *"As near as I can figure it, every word I used in turning Woolworth down has cost me about a million dollars!"* [49]

Take Opportunities As They Arise!

___

[49] http://www.sermonillustrations.com/a-z/o/opportunity.htm

Take the well-known experience of Edward Lowe back in the 1940s. He was in the business of producing a clay-based material that would soak up oil and grease spills. One day a neighbour asked to try the compound in her cat box. Lowe's product didn't track all over the house, and didn't look too bad. Lowe realized he was on to something and he began selling the compound to pet shops. He went on to supply 40% of the $400-million per year cat-box filler market. *Take Opportunities As They Arise!*

Almost every great movement forward in history has been a result of insightful and courageous people *Taking Opportunities As They Arise!* Abraham Lincoln nobly *Took The Opportunity* of civil division and greater education within the U.S. to end the practice of slavery. Martin Luther King Jr. legitimately *Took The Opportunity* of major cultural and demographic shifts in America in the 1960s to make significant strides towards racial equality and human rights. Nelson Mandela stood strong and *Took The Opportunity* of world-wide support for his cause of freedom from racial oppression and abuse, to right the decades of wrongs of apartheid.

The truth is that we either seize the moment or we are seized by the moments & events around us. *Carpe Diem!* Much of life, and building success in life, is about learning not to be controlled by events, but about influencing and seizing events yourself. *Take Opportunities As They Arise!*

3-Legged Stool For Taking Opportunities:

There is a *3-Legged Stool for Taking Opportunities*. If any one of the legs of the stool is missing, the stool will collapse and the *Opportunity* is missed:

1) Live Your **LIFEFIT**

2) Resist Opportunity Thieves

3) Seeing & Seizing Opportunity

3-Legged Stool For Taking Opportunities:

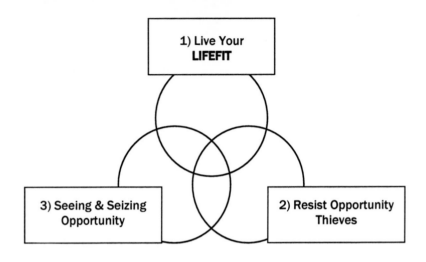

1) Live Your *LIFEFIT*

The first leg of the **3-Legged Stool for Taking Opportunities** is actually making a determined choice on a daily basis to **Live Your LIFEFIT**, and following through on that choice every day, no matter what. Actually **Living Your LIFEFIT** puts you in a position to have **Opportunities** open themselves up to you.

See, *Opportunity knocks when we build a door for Opportunity to knock on!* We build this door by **Living Our LIFEFIT**. The closer we live in alignment to our **LIFEFIT**, the more visible our door is for *Opportunity* to knock on. I mentioned this earlier, but it is worth mentioning again. Bono of U2 said: *"I judge where we are by how close I am to the melody I'm hearing in my head, and how close are we to what we can do as a band to realizing our potential."*[50] This is reminiscent of Oliver Wendell Holmes, who said: *"Many people die with their music still in*

---

[50] Assayas, Michka, *Bono In Conversation With Michka Assayas,* The Berkley Publishing Group, New York, New York, 2005, p.41

them. Why is this so? Too often it is because they are always getting ready to live. Before they know it, time runs out."[51] True success is playing close to the melody and music and art within... it is realizing our personal potential... it is *Getting Where You Need To Go. Getting Where You Need To Go* is all about your personal Life Mission; realizing your personal potential; **Living Your LIFEFIT:**

L – Learning About Your **Passions**

I – Investigating Your **Personality**

F – Finding Out Your **Gifts & Abilities**

E – Exploring & Clarifying Your **Mission**

F – Facilitating & Developing **Marketable Skills**

I – Including **Networking & Relationships**

T– Taking **Opportunities** As They Arise

Milton Berle said, *"If opportunity doesn't knock, build a door."*[52] We build this door when we *Live Our* **LIFEFIT**. When we live in a way that is congruent with our **LIFEFIT**; when we live in alignment with our **LIFEFIT**, we put ourselves in a position where *Opportunity* can knock on our door regularly!

One last thought here. There is an Indian saying that goes like this: "When you were born, you cried and the world rejoiced. Live your life in such a manner that when you die the world cries and you rejoice." *Live Your* **LIFEFIT**, and the world will rejoice, and then cry when you pass on.

---

[51] http://raymondmarr.com/carpe-diem-quotes-seize-the-day-sayings-life
[52] http://www.brainyquote.com/quotes/authors/m/milton_berle.html

2) Resist Opportunity Thieves

One day this past summer, my 10-year old son Joshua had a tough day. It didn't start out that way. Actually, it started our great because we were going fishing. Josh absolutely loves fishing. Most of the fishing we do is very simple, very small scale, and it's catch and release. But still, Josh just loves the thrill of the catch and sitting on a dock or the shore or on a boat and casting away, and reeling in. And I love it because I get to spend time with him.

As we were fishing, Josh had a bite. You could tell by the action on the rod that it was fairly significant, and so my friend Blair and I began to work with Josh to reel it in. Josh's sister Julie was all excited, and you could see by the huge smile on Josh's face that today for him was about to be complete. Today was gonna to be a good day!

So he reeled the fish in to within 2-3 feet from the shore. We could all see the fish fighting away. He was a decent size, about 10-12 inches. Right at the shore, when we had the net out and were about to scoop him up, he broke free of the line and swam away.

A small tear appeared in the corner of Josh's eye, and I could tell he was pretty upset. I tried to comfort him. The fish fought so hard because he thought he was fighting for his life. We were simply fighting for the pleasure of the catch. But Josh was sad. This fish was *the one that got away.*

Many of us live with the pain of regret. Benjamin Franklin said, *"Most people die at 25... and wait until they are 75 to be buried."* We need to be so careful that we are not walking around, dead at 25, or 35, or 55, waiting until we are 75 to be buried. We need to live our lives today in such away that we live without regret. We do so by Resisting Opportunity Thieves!

There are many *Opportunity Thieves* that we need to *Resist.*

Opportunity Thieves <u>minimize</u> the value of *Opportunities* that knock on our door, and *<u>minimize</u>* the *Opportunity Cost* of letting *Opportunities* walk away.

They also *maximize* the *Cost of the Opportunity* so it seems way too difficult for us to *Take Opportunities* as they arise.

See, every *Opportunity* has an *Opportunity Cost*, and there is a *Cost For Every Opportunity*:

The *Opportunity Cost* – What it costs to walk away from an *Opportunity*...

The *Cost Of The Opportunity* – What it costs to pursue an *Opportunity*...

Opportunity Thieves minimize the value of *Opportunities* knocking on our door, and minimize the *Opportunity Cost* of letting *Opportunities* walk away, and maximize the *Cost of the Opportunity* so that it seems too costly for us to pursue *Opportunities* as they arise. Three Common *Opportunity Thieves* include:

Distractions – Abraham Lincoln said, *"In the end, it's not the years in your life that count. It's the life in your years."* In other words, what is most important is not how long you lived, but how you lived the years that you had. Some with amazing talent, ability and personality never really live in alignment with their **LIFEFIT**, simply because they are so distracted with the business of living and pleasure and having a good time. We need to enjoy life and have fun while we are here, but balance that with not being distracted from ***Living Our* LIFEFIT** and *Taking Opportunities As They Arise!*

Poor Time Management – Henry David Thoreau famously said some words that have stuck in my mind for a long time: *"As if you could kill time without injuring eternity."* Gulp. So many times, I have said or heard something said that, at the time, is very casual and simple: "I will just kill some time until…" The time we kill has no resurrection. We can never get it back. We will discuss time management in greater detail a little later, but we should be careful that the *Opportunities* that present themselves to us are not stolen because we do not properly use or allocate the time we have.

Fear – I love this quote from Mary Manin Morrissey: *"You block your dream when you allow your fear to grow bigger than your faith."* [53] Fear is a significant *Opportunity Thief* because

---

[53] http://www.quotegarden.com/fear.html

when it grows larger than our dream, it holds us back from achieving the things we really want to achieve, and it holds us back from *Taking Opportunities As They Arise*. The value of experience is not only wrinkles, but in time you see that most of the things you feared never came true. Most of what we have stress and anxiety over never really happens. But it is easier to live in fear than it is to live in faith. Don't allow the Opportunities that arise to be stolen by fear. No one on their deathbed ever says things like, *"I wish I had been more afraid, I wish I had listened to my fear, I wish I had never taken any risks, I wish I had lived a more stressful, anxious, worried life."* If people regret anything, it is living in fear. People generally do not regret living a life that brims over with faith.

3) "See" & "Seize" Opportunity

The 3rd leg **Seeing & Seizing Opportunity**. Roy D. Chapin Jr. said: *"Be ready when opportunity comes... Luck is the time when preparation and opportunity meet."* In other words, what looks like luck, is often people who are actually prepared when Opportunity comes and knocks on their door. Learning to SEE Opportunity is the first step, because you have to see it before you see it!

Learn To "SEE" Opportunity...

Develop A Positive Attitude – Believe *"it"* will happen to YOU! When we have an optimistic attitude of faith and belief, we expand our range of vision to SEE the *Opportunities* and good things right in front of us! Harry Truman said, *"A pessimist is one who makes difficulties of his opportunities and an optimist is one who makes opportunities of his difficulties."* Maybe the *Opportunity* has been right in front of you all along, but you either didn't believe in yourself, or saw it simply as a problem or difficulty. The reality is that if you have a dream, but are without a positive attitude, you are simply a daydreamer. On the other hand, a person with positive attitude absent a dream produces a pleasant person who can't make progress. A dream teamed up with a positive attitude produces a person with unlimited possibilities, vast **Opportunity**, and limitless potential. As Donald Trump says, *"As long as you're going to be thinking anyway, think big."*

Open Your Perspective – At times we miss *Seeing Opportunity* because we decide where the *Opportunity* should come from. Don't judge where or how or through whom Opportunity will come! In my own life, *Opportunity* has often come through channels that surprised me:

- Personal Pain
- Difficult People
- Financial Hardship
- Injustice
- Personal Failure
- Broken Structures
- Broken Situations
- Dire Straits

Opportunity will knock through whichever channel it wants to!

Look For Congruence & Alignment – Congruence and alignment are more look and feel than exact science. It is hard to quantify exactly when to jump in and go after something. But you will learn and grow and begin to know. It's like surfing. You need to see the waves begin to roll, and feel the movement and texture of the water. However, when the *"stars begin to line up"*, when the *"buds begin to bloom"*, when the *"pot starts to boil"*, you will learn. You will know. You will grow. You will respond and act!

Now that we **SEE** the *Opportunity*, how can we learn to **SEIZE** the *Opportunity*? It is far more painful to miss an *Opportunity* you know you missed because you **SEE** the *Opportunity*, than it is to miss an *Opportunity* you never **SAW**. How can we **SEIZE** *Opportunities* that come our way?

Learn To "SEIZE" Opportunity...

Prepare! – When we are prepared for *Opportunity*, we are generally able to take advantage of *Opportunities* as they arise. This is extremely practical. Think of it like the ant preparing for winter. Stock-pile today whatever you think will be necessary for *Opportunity* tomorrow. Get out of debt as quickly as you can, set aside some cash reserve, and stock-pile education, training, certification, relationships, networks; whatever you could possibly need to *Take Opportunities As They Arise*. Remember, it wasn't raining when Noah started building the ark!

Be Bold! – I call this **"First Strike Capability"**. When an *Opportunity* arises, a measure of boldness is generally called for. We need to radically resist our fears and strike while the iron is hot. Be bold!

Invest! – It's going to cost you, one way or the other. Do a CBA– Cost-Benefit Analysis". This is where you weigh the costs of an action (or inaction) against the benefits of that same action (or inaction). The cost of an *Opportunity* is often outweighed by the *Opportunity* cost of not taking advantage of the *Opportunity*. Don't let the price scare you. If we are not prepared to invest in *Opportunities* we may have a return on that non-investment of regret and discouragement.

Work Hard! – Thomas Edison famously said, *"Opportunity is missed by most people because it is dressed in overalls and looks like work"*. Isn't that the humble truth. No **Opportunity** was ever seized by a person who was struggling to get out of bed. We can only grab the Opportunity around us when we are awake, alert, and coherent.

The key is **Living Your LIFEFIT**. Living in a way that is aligned and congruent with our **LIFEFIT** is healthy and holistic! Live in a way that flows with your *Passions, Personality, Gifts & Abilities,* and your *Personal Mission.* Top them all off with Facilitating & Developing *Marketable Skills.* Include *Networking & Relationships.* Relationships are a crucial key in unlocking your destiny. And lastly, ***Take Opportunities As They Arise.*** Be prepared to SEE and then SEIZE the Opportunities the Universe brings your way. Helen Keller said, *"One can never consent to creep when one feels an impulse to soar."* We may find it difficult to soar if we don't take advantage of the Opportunity the wind presents us with!

Let's review our progress so far. Fill in the blanks:

Living My *L.I.F.E.F.I.T.:*

<u>L</u> – *Learning About* Your ***Passions*** – My *Passions* Are:

_____

_____

_____

<u>I</u> – *Investigating* Your ***Personality*** – My *Personality* Is:

_____

_____

_____

<u>F</u> – *Finding Out* Your ***Gifts & Abilities*** – My *Gifts & Abilities* Are:_____

_____

_____

_____

134

E – *Exploring* & Clarifying Your *Mission* – My *Mission* Is:

_____

_____

_____

F – *Facilitating* & Developing *Marketable Skills* – My *Marketable Skills* Are :

_____

_____

_____

_____

_____

I – *Including Networking & Relationships* – My *Network* Includes:

_____

_____

_____

_____

T – *Taking Opportunities* As They Arise – My *Opportunities* Are:

_____

_____

_____

"L.I.F.E.F.I.T." Matrix

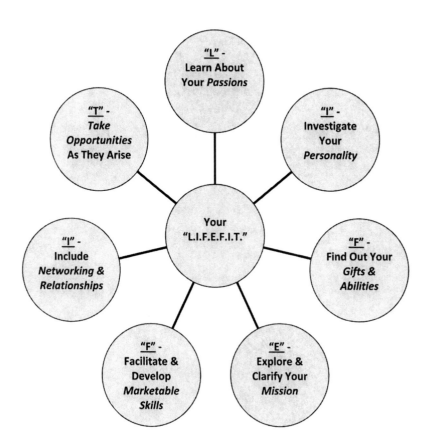

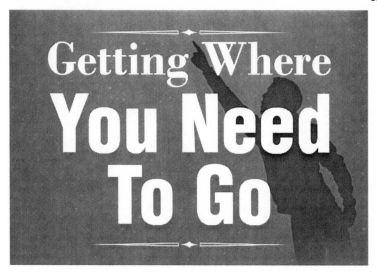

Part 2

There Is A *"How"*

*"What's the use of running
if you're not on the right road?"*

German Proverb

Getting Where You Need To Go
Chapter 11 – Getting There:
The Power Of Your Choices

Now that we have moved into Part 2, we are in a different phase in *Getting Where You Need To Go*.

Part 1 looked at the amazing reality that each and every one of us has a "Why" and a "Where"… a purpose for our existence and a place we need to go. This "Why" and "Where" was defined as our **LIFEFIT**. *Getting Where You Need To Go* is all about your personal "Why" *and* "Where"... your **LIFEFIT**:

L – Learning About Your **Passions**

I – Investigating Your **Personality**

F – Finding Out Your **Gifts & Abilities**

E – Exploring & Clarifying Your **Mission**

F – Facilitating & Developing **Marketable Skills**

I – Including **Networking & Relationships**

T – Taking **Opportunities** As They Arise

Now we transition to the "How". If I am clear about Why I Am Here and Where I Need To Go, the natural next question is How Do I Get There? *Getting Where You Need To Go* is not about the theoretical or the realm of fantasy; it is about the practical and the reality.

See, *Getting Where You Need To Go* and Living Your **LIFEFIT** is about living your dreams. In the movie Braveheart, there is a moment where William Wallace, the Scottish freedom fighter, says: *"Every man dies. But not every man truly lives."* We *truly live* when we are living our dreams. A dream is a picture painted on the inside of your heart that reveals a glimpse of the potential stored within you. *Dreams are accurate indicators and powerful reflections of your actual growth potential.* But HOW do we get there?

We get there by *making choices*. All of us come from different parts of the world, with different cultures, upbringing, education and experiences which have shaped us. We have lived through sunshine and rain, blessing and cursing, joys and sorrows, events that have healed and events that have hurt. We all have different perspectives and unique spirituality, distinct personalities and tastes, diverse gifts and abilities. But one thing we can agree on is the power we have all been given to make choices and thus have a direct impact and influence on our destiny.

The Power Of Our Choices

There was a time in my life when I really believed I was powerless and not *really* responsible for where I was and where I was going. Having experienced my share of pain in the first 15 years of my life, I really believed I simply was what I was and could not genuinely change.

I was shaped at an early age primarily by abandonment, lack of affection, and abuse. As a result, I wrestled with un-met emotional needs, and was desperately crying out for affirmation, attention, and affection. I remember feeling overwhelming loneliness again and again as a child and teenager, even though I had a decent group of friends. Thus there was an internal barrenness and fear of rejection, along with a fear of being abandoned.

This left me in a place of insecurity and internal torment, and as a result, I made some unhealthy choices. However, these were choices I felt a certain level of powerlessness about. I felt like I wanted to make different choices; healthy choices, but continually made unhealthy choices. I went for counselling. With my own background as a counsellor, I could understand some of the root causes behind my unhealthy choices. I could clearly see why I was pursuing things I really didn't want to pursue.

However, this knowledge was almost a negative thing because for some time, I used it as an excuse for failure. I told myself: *"Well of course you do* this and that; of course you feel this way and that way; of course you think those thoughts…you were abandoned by your own father at age 2, and the significant primary relationships in your life caused you deep levels of pain and were at times, even abusive." For me, this knowledge didn't so much empower me as give me an excuse, and I took on victim mentality.

Thankfully, this did not last long. I felt like a victim, like I was owed something. I felt as though I was blameless for what I was doing and that others were to blame. I had become a prisoner of my past, rather than an architect of my future. Then one day, I read that famous quote of Mark Twain: *"Don't go around saying the world owes you a living. The world owes you nothing. It was here first."* I realized that though I knew I was here for a special purpose, I was not living like it.

I fell into the trap of our victim culture, where everyone else is to blame *except* me. Sadly, pop culture sometimes makes it easy for us to duck responsibility. Rather than a humility and sense of personal responsibility, and empowerment, the incredible levels of self-awareness that Oprah and Dr.Phil and the pervasive self-help culture have created has often led to a *blame culture* and *lack of personal responsibility*. We need a new sense of empowerment around our ability to make choices and thus determine our own destiny. Our destiny is not determined by chance but by choice. In the 2007 U.S. Presidential Election, Barack Obama said: *"Change will not come if we wait for some other person or some other time. We are the ones we've been waiting for. We are the change that we seek."* The immediate consequence of being an adult is we get to write our own ticket. The crucial key to personal transformation is simply personal choice!

For me, this knowledge was a turning point. I realized that my life today is not the sum total of what has happened to me and what has been said to me, but it is the sum total of the choices I have made. I began to be empowered, and though every choice I made did not lead to instant results, when I stuck with them and planned my steps, I experienced more success than failure. And I have discovered that in the realm of *Getting Where You Need To Go*, there are 3 choices we need to make, that will help us, perhaps more than others:

- The Choice To *Work Hard,*
- The Choice To *Continually Grow,*
- The Choice To *Persevere*

$$HW + CG + P = R$$

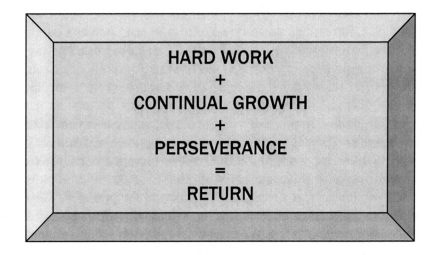

1) *The Choice To Work Hard*

The tragedy of studying about *Gifts & Abilities* is that for some, it gives them an excuse to be lazy and not put out the amount of effort and hard work necessary for lasting success. No matter how talented we may be, no matter how gifted, there is never a substitute for *hard work.* Michelangelo said, *"If people only knew how hard I work to gain my mastery, it wouldn't seem so wonderful at all."* What an honest admission from one of history's most talented artists!

I am a big believer in "working smart", but in the whole conversation about "working smart", one of the most important principles for success in any endeavour is often overlooked, and that is "working hard". Principles don't wear out, fade out, or break down. They last forever. They are timeless, tireless, and ageless. Principles cannot be used too much. Life is the process of discovering principles – of discovering what works and what doesn't. If you want to make rapid progress and achieve lasting success, don't fight against principles – flow with them. And the principle of "working hard" is crucial.

No dream ever comes true until you wake up and go to work. There's a process for *Getting Where You Need To Go* and Living Your **LIFEFIT**. Many of us start goals and projects but don't complete them. We have great dreams but seldom fulfill them. This is partly because we don't get results fast enough. We work hard for a time, but the effort we put in is greater than the results we get back at the start, so we quit!

See, success reinforces progress. It encourages us to keep going. Without it, our confidence starts to fade. This is the principle of, *"Effort And Return"*. With anything new, you have to build momentum. You have to invest more at the beginning than you get out of it. The reward or return comes later. In all you do, you are making an investment, putting in more time and energy at the start. If we can hang on through the initial period of greater investment, we will see the return and results.

To be blessed in the things you do and have success, work hard! Inevitably, diligent people want and get, while lazy people want but do not get. The ancient book of Proverbs, chapter 13 and verse 4 instructs us wisely: *"The soul of the sluggard craves and gets nothing; But the soul of the diligent is made fat."* The *key to wanting and getting is to* "working hard". The sluggard craves, he desires and he gets nothing…

"Sluggard" – to be averse to activity, effort, or movement; habitually lazy, to be slack, to lean idly.

"Craves" – to wish for, eager desire, to long for, to want, to desire *natural things such as food, drink, etc.*.

"Diligent" – characterized by steady, earnest, and energetic application and effort, painstaking, persevering application.

"Made Fat" – to be fat, to fatten, to satisfy, to be well fed, to be rich and mighty. Fat animals were considered to be the most healthy, therefore the concept of prosperity was associated with fatness.

Diligent people want and get. Lazy people want... but get nothing. Those who are diligent, who are "hard working" and who are characterized by steady, earnest, and energetic application and effort will become prosperous!! Those who are lazy, who are sluggards and spend a lot of time *"leaning around"* will want but get nothing. Even their natural desires will not fulfilled.

Outcomes of Hard Work...

- Wealth
- Personal Growth
- Promotion
- Satisfied Desires
- You Get Ahead

Outcomes of Laziness...

- Personal Stagnation
- Demotion
- Constant Dissatisfaction
- You Never Get Ahead
- Poverty

Self-Assessment Questions Regarding Your Work Habits...

- Do I genuinely work hard?
- Am I regarded by others as a hard worker?
- Am I on time at least 90% of the time?
- Do I complete projects on time, at least 90% of the time?
- Do I go the extra mile when needed?
- Do I manage time well?

- If I quit, could my boss give me a reference that would get me hired?
- If the boss could only give one employee a raise, would it be me?
- Can I honestly say I work as hard for my boss as I would if_____(someone you admire) was my boss?

2) *The Choice To Continually Grow*

Fundamentally, every one of us is destined for something great. The potential within every one of us is staggering and without limit. What is within you is far greater than everything that has come against you. We cannot allow the *gap* between our *current performance* and our *full potential* to discourage us from seeing or forgetting about that *full potential*. Dale Carnegie said it like this: *"We all have possibilities we don't know about. We can do things we don't even dream we can do."*

However, we will not reach our potential by staying the way we are. We will only reach our potential by engaging in a process of *continual growth*. We do not so much *"achieve"* our potential, as *"grow into"* it.

There is far more in you than you have let out up until now. Richard E. Boyd said, *"Few men during their lifetime come anywhere near exhausting the resources within them. There are deep wells of strength that are seldom used."* The only way these *"deep wells of strength"* get utilized is through training and continual growth. Before greatness can come, we need to train for it. The *depth* of our *preparation* determines the *height* of our *destiny*.

- ⊙ *The Shorter Our Training, The Shorter Our Destiny*

- ⊙ *The Smaller Our Training, The Smaller Our Destiny*

- ⊙ *The Deeper Our Training, The Higher Our Destiny*

- ⊙ *The Greater Our Training, The Broader Our Destiny*

⊙ *The More Thorough Our Training, The Richer Our Destiny*

⊙ *Time In Training = Strength In Reigning*

The reality is that right now, you are in training for the next level in your life. You are training *personally* today for your *personal* level tomorrow. You are training *relationally* today for your *relational* level tomorrow. You are training in your *career* today for your *career* level tomorrow. You are training *mentally* and *emotionally* today for your *mental* and *emotional* level tomorrow. We are always in training for the next level.

The Progression Goes Like This:

a) *We Begin To Grasp Our* **LIFEFIT** and *Where We Need To Go*, then…

b) *Training – Growth and then* testing *to gauge our learning*, then…

c) *We Pass Or Fail The Test, Or Come Somewhere In The Middle*, then…

d) *Advancement To A New Level or Go Back For More Training*

We need to create a *Training Environment* and culture of *continual growth* in our lives. Who you are today is not all you can be. There is truly no greater tragedy than *"I could have been…"*. Most of us think that successful people in life are simply lucky. But I believe that what looks like *"luck"* is more often people who work hard and are ready for an opportunity when it arises. Oprah Winfrey said, *"Luck is a matter of preparation meeting opportunity."* When we prepare for the opportunities in our lives, it often looks like overnight success, but in reality it is the results of years of hard work. To realize our full potential we need to work, we need to train, prepare, and commit to *continual growth. Lots of people want to be a skyscraper in life but only have the foundation of a woodshed!*

Preparation & Training Is Essential...

"I hated every minute of the training, but I said, 'Don't quit. Suffer now and live the rest of your life as a champion.'" - *Muhammad Ali*

"In business or in football, it takes a lot of unspectacular preparation to produce spectacular results." - *Roger Staubach*

"Unless a person has trained himself for his chance, the chance will only make him ridiculous. A great occasion is worth to man exactly what his preparation enables him to make of it." - *J.B. Matthews*

So, how do we create a *Training Environment* and culture of *continual growth* in our lives? Well, **IRREVERSIBLE LIFE PRINCIPLE # 1** is that *we reap what we sow*. No one can change this. The bottom line in life is that you reap what you sow. I am experiencing today what I caused yesterday, either by action or inaction. *We are all sowing seeds at all times. The question is: what are we sowing?* I know today the seeds of knowledge I planted yesterday. If we sow training and continual growth, we will reap a fruitful life.

Daily Plan For Personal Growth:

🔎 *What Will I Read? What Information Do I Need To Gather?* Devote yourself to reading, if you are a natural or not. Leaders who consistently read grow more and are *fresher* than leaders who don't. Set a goal to read at least 1 book per month, progressing to 1 every two weeks, and then 1 per week. Devote 15-20 minutes daily to reading to grow your knowledge base.

🔎 *Where Can I Feed?* What Attitudes & Concepts Do I Need Which Will Elevate My Thinking In Ways That Will Empower Me To Move Forward? Devote a tithe, 10% of your waking hours to spending time feeding your mind, your concepts, your belief system. Knowledge = Power.

🔎 *What Do I Need To Weed?* What Attitudes, Beliefs and Thoughts Do I Wrestle With Which Hinder Me From Continual Growth?

🔎 *Where Should I Seed?* Where Do I Need To Invest and Sow Seeds (time, money, good will, help and assistance) In The Lives Of Others? Constantly sow seeds into the lives of others. True prosperity is having enough to meet your needs, as well as the needs of others.

🔎 *Where Can I Lead?* As We Step Out And Lead Others, We Grow. There is no greater exercise to strengthen the heart than to reach down and lift someone else higher.

🔎 *How Will I Bleed?* Difficult Times, Difficult People, and Personal Pain are tremendous sources of personal growth, if we walk through them with the mindset of a student, and with dignity, grace, gratitude. We grow more through pain than almost through any other avenue. The question is HOW will we walk through it? What choice will make in regards to our mindset?

3) *The Choice To Persevere*

Perseverance is the key to accomplishments, both great and small. George Allen said, *"People of mediocre ability sometimes achieve outstanding success because they don't know when to quit. Most men succeed because they are determined to.* [54]

Perseverance is simply pushing through obstacles. It is about outlasting every obstacle, barrier and enemy. There are negative energies, obstacles, circumstances, and sometimes even people that will fight your dream. Don't be intimidated or surprised by them. Simply win! Overcome! Outlast every opponent and obstacle with your dogged perseverance. Be like a bulldog! As they said in the movie "Forrest Gump": *"Run, Forrest, Run!"*

- Dr. Seuss's first children's book was rejected by 23 publishers. The 24th publisher sold 6 million,

- During their first year of business, Coca-Cola sold only 400 Cokes,

- In his first 3 years in the car business, Henry Ford went bankrupt twice,

- Michael Jordan was cut from his high school basketball team,

- Wayne Gretzky was considered too small and slow to play in the NHL,

- In 1905, the University of Bern rejected a Ph.D. dissertation, saying it was irrelevant & fanciful. Albert Einstein was down but not defeated,

- Frank Woolworth laboured to save his first $50, and then saw 3 of his first 5 chain stores fail.

John D. Rockefeller said, *"I do not think there is any other quality so essential to success of any kind as the quality of perseverance. It overcomes almost everything, even nature".* We need to persevere, to hang in there. Soon, light will come at the

---

[54] http://www.abundance-and-happiness.com/perseverance-quotes.html

end of the tunnel. By perseverance the snail reached the ark! Calvin Coolidge, the 30th President of the United States, said this:

> *"Nothing in the world can take the place of persistence. Talent will not; nothing is more common than unsuccessful men with talent. Genius will not; un-rewarded genius is almost a proverb. Education alone will not; the world is full of educated failures. Persistence and determination alone are omnipotent."*

No matter what the obstacle, struggle, or barrier, persevere! *We know we have* persevered *enough when we achieve what we set out to achieve!*

Producing Perseverance:

- **Fuel Your Tank** – Take time to fuel your personal energy levels with healthy diet and regular exercise. It is amazing how connected the health of our body is to our ability to keep on keeping on!

- **Rest Your Mind, Body and Spirit** – Take time to get healthy amounts of sleep, relaxation, and recreation. It only makes sense that this will help us to persevere and press on!

- **Remember Your Why** – When the battle is on in full swing, and every indication is that you should quit, take a moment to remind yourself of your Why, your **LIFEFIT**, and *Where You Need To Go.*

- **Surround Yourself With Positive Support** – Make sure the people who say you can't, you shouldn't, and you couldn't have no platform to speak into your life. Surround yourself will those who have positive energy.

- **Continue To Make The Choice To Persevere** – Keep on keeping on until you *Get Where You Need To Go…* until you are Living Your **LIFEFIT**… until your journey feels complete. Enough said.

We are transitioning to the "How". If I am clear about *Why I Am Here* and *Where I Need To Go*, the natural next question is *How Do I Get There? Getting Where You Need To Go* is not about the theoretical or a fantasy, it is about the practical and the reality. In *Getting Where You Need To Go*, there are 3 choices we need to make on a regular basis:

The Choice To Work Hard,

The Choice To Continually Grow,

The Choice To Persevere

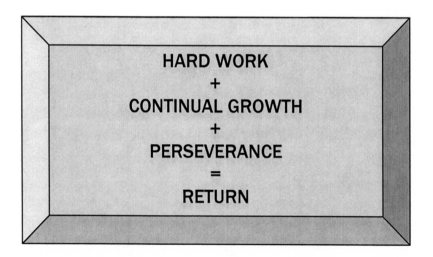

HARD WORK
+
CONTINUAL GROWTH
+
PERSEVERANCE
=
RETURN

Remember the process on the road to fulfilling your dream. *Hard work, continual growth,* and *perseverance* always bring a return! There is no such thing as *"all of the sudden success"*, or *"overnight success"*, except AFTER a long period of hard work! The qualities will facilitate us as we seek to *Get Where We Need To Go*… until we are *Living Our* **LIFEFIT.**

Getting Where You Need To Go
Chapter 12 – *Getting There:*
Managing The Moments

In Part 2, we're in a different phase in *Getting Where You Need To Go*. In Part 1 we saw that each one of us has a "Why" and a "Where"… a purpose for our existence, and a place we need to go. This "Why" and "Where" is our **LIFEFIT**:

L – Learning About Your **Passions**

I – Investigating Your **Personality**

F – Finding Out Your **Gifts** & **Abilities**

E – Exploring & Clarifying Your **Mission**

F – Facilitating & Developing **Marketable Skills**

I – Including **Networking** & **Relationships**

T – Taking **Opportunities** As They Arise

Now we transition to the *"How"*. If I am clear about *Why I Am Here* and *Where I Need To Go*, the natural next question is *How Do I Get There? Getting Where You Need To Go* is not just about the dreaming, but the doing. *Getting Where You Need To Go* and Living Your **LIFEFIT** is about living your dreams. *Dreams are powerful reflections of your actual growth potential.* But HOW do we take our potential and make it actual?

We get there by making choices. And we *Get Where We Need To Go* by learning to **Manage The Moments**. Our success or failure, when it comes to *Getting Where We Need To Go,* often revolves around how well we *Manage The Moments. Getting Where You Need To Go* is not just about strengths, gifts, ability, passion, or talent. It's about *Managing The Moments. Managing The Moments* is key to life. Benjamin Franklin said, *"Dost thou love life? Then do not squander time; for that's the stuff life is made of".* Our life is made up of the stuff called time!

Managing The Moments – Every Day Is Doomsday!

Ralph Waldo Emerson wrote, *"One of the illusions of life is that the present hour is not the critical, decisive hour. Write it on your heart that every day is the best day in the year. No man has learned anything rightly, until he knows that every day is Doomsday"* [55]. WOW! No one has learned anything properly until they know that every day is Doomsday.

"Doomsday" sounds so scary, but thinking of it in those terms reinforces the importance of *Managing The Moments* and living your life with a sense of urgency. Imagine what your life would look like if you lived it with that kind of urgency. Imagine having the sense that every day was Doomsday, that every hour was crucial, that every minute was valuable, that every moment was decisive. Imagine where you could go, what you could achieve, who you could meet, what you could do! Imagine what you could squeeze out and pull off if you really Managed The Moments.

In reality, until we have the deep sense in our heart of hearts of the importance of time, we may not give it the required sense of urgency. A sense of urgency goes hand in hand with *Managing The Moments*. I cannot overstate the importance of urgency. For us to *Get Where We Need To Go*, Live Our **LIFEFIT**, and have no regrets, urgency is required. No one has learned anything rightly until they understand that every day is Doomsday!

I heard this quote years ago from Jim Rohn, a leading motivational speaker. As I continue on my personal journey, I can see its truth more clearly with each passing day: *"We must all suffer from one of two pains: the pain of discipline or the pain of regret. The difference is discipline weighs ounces while regret weighs tons."* If you live without the urgency to *Manage The Moments* and *Get Where You Need To Go*, you might regret it. As the years slip away and you realize all you could have been, all you could have done, and all you could have accomplished, the pain of regret could be overwhelming.

---

[55] Derrick Sweet, 2002, *"Healthy Wealthy and Wise"*, Toronto, Ont.: The Healthy Wealthy & Wise Corporation, p.77

The urgency we are speaking about to *Manage The Moments* flows from a genuine sense that your time and your *Moments* equals your life. Therefore, when we waste our time, we waste our life. However, when we *Manage The Moments*, we manage our lives in a healthy way. Your *time* = your life; therefore, when you waste your time, you waste your life. When you master your time, you master your life. As Stephen Covey said, *"The key is in not spending time, but in investing it."* We are writing the story of our lives, one Moment at a time.

Truths About Time

1) *Time Is A Gift*

People who live with a sense that time is a gift are more likely to treat their time with respect and *Manage Their Moments* effectively, than those who do not live with this sense. Perhaps this is because gratitude is a gift that empowers us to respect and value that which we are grateful for.

Every day is a gift which has been given to us, and every *Moment* we have to *Manage* is an endowment to our lives. The good moments and the bad, the easy moments and the hard, the moments we celebrate and the moments we shed tears. They are *all* gifts. We never know when the time we are given will no longer be given to us. So, let's treat is as a gift and honour it appropriately, *Managing The Moments* with care, gratitude, and respect. Time is perhaps the most valuable gift you've been given!

2) *Time Is A Tangible Resource*

The ancient Hebrews had a proverb that went like this:

> *"Seventy years are given to us! Some may even reach eighty... Teach us to make the most of our time, so that we may grow in wisdom."* [56]

The truth is that if we saw our time in the same way we see our money, many of us would probably work to *"spend"* it wisely. Something interesting happens when we have cash in our wallet or in our bank account and we are faced with an opportunity to *spend* it: we do an internal mini "CBA" – a *Cost Benefit Analysis*. We decide if the money we are about to *spend* is worth the *benefit* we will gain from what we are spending it on. We weigh the *cost* against the *benefit* and ask if one outweighs the other. We know how hard we worked to earn the money, and so we need to assure ourselves that what we will receive in return will be appropriate compensation.

What a personal revolution would occur if we treated our time the same way! If we looked at our time as a tangible resource, like cash in our jeans, and carefully weighed the benefits of a certain action before we spent our time on it! This is a crucial key in effectively *Managing The Moments*! Time is a tangible resource!

3) *Time Is A Valuable Resource*

To quote from that proverb again: *"Teach us to make the most of our time, so that we may grow in wisdom"*. This teaches us that we arrive at wisdom when we make the most of our time. *Managing The Moments = Growth In Wisdom.*

Think about this with me. If a person was handed millions of dollars, an embarrassment of wealth, and totally squandered it,

---

[56] *Holy Bible, New Living Translation*, (Wheaton, IL: Tyndale House Publishers, Inc.) 1996

what would you say? Let's say they won several million dollars in the lottery, or discovered a rich uncle who left them millions in their will. Let's say they took the money and blew all of it on absolutely wasteful, useless, extravagant spending. Not one drop of the money went to their family, or any assets that would last, or any worthy cause.

It all went down the drain. You wouldn't tell their story in the context of , *"I heard about this really brilliant and wise person who…"* Mostly likely, you would say something like, *"I heard about this idiot who received all this money and completely blew it."* Careful and well thought-through management and stewardship generally equates itself with wisdom. Careless spending is only thought of as foolish.

Benjamin Franklin was the one who said, as he gave advice to a young tradesmen, *"Time is money"*. The incredible worth of our time can be seen when we realize that lost Time can never be found again - you can only spend it once. John Randolph said, *"When you kill time, remember that it has no resurrection"*. When you *"spend"* your time, you can never get it back.

This motivates us to *Manage The Moments* well. As a matter of fact, I would go so far as to say that time is more valuable than money. I can spend money and normally get it back quickly, but when I use my time, the moment is gone forever. This is further impetus to Manage The Moments well.

4) *Time Passes More Quickly Than You Think*

Tragically, we so often do not realize how quickly time passes until we have very little left. As an ordained minister who spent 12 years providing pastoral care to congregations, I spent my fair share of time at the deathbed.

I discovered over those years and in those moments that the deathbed is a place of truth. As I would sit with the dying, I would listen as the person spoke of all their regrets and the things they wished they had done or wished they had said. I never heard anyone wish they had spent more time on their smart phone or wish they had worked more or spent more time at the office. I never listened in as people lamented not making more money or not getting more promotions.

But more than once, people grieved over not spending the time to say the loving and caring things they wanted to say to their loved ones. They grieved over being distracted from time with their family and friends. And I saw tears over lives lived, but dreams unfulfilled. I saw the sadness as a person reflected on how they had missed the opportunity to **Live Their** LIFEFIT, and *Get Where They Needed To Go.*

The tragedy was hearing, time and time again: *"I thought I had more time."* It is extremely rare to hear of people who felt they had too much time. Much more common is meeting those who felt they did not have enough time, and thought they would have had more time to do and to say all the things they wanted to do and to say.

This is a challenge to all of us to *Manage The Moments* well, because time passes much more quickly than we think!

5) *Time Can Either Be Spent Building The "Tent" Or The "Temple"*

People spend their time building *tents* when they could be building *temples*. In other words, so many spend their time on the temporary when they could be spending their time building a legacy.

See, some things that we do in this life are temporary; they are perishable. They have a *"best before"* date, and only last short periods of time, and benefit mainly ourselves: *"building the tent"*, so to speak. Other things we spend our time on are legacy items, things which last for significant periods of time and benefit others: *"building the temple"*, so to speak. The difference is mainly in the focus around temporary and personal benefit versus those things which last and benefit others. Let's examine our focus...

Building A Tent...	Building A Temple...
Temporary Items	Legacy Items
Short Lasting	Long Lasting
Best Before Date	No Expiry Date
Short-Term Pleasures	Long-Term Gains
Today Oriented	Tomorrow Oriented
For The Now	For The Future
Getting Through Today	Planning For Tomorrow
Benefit To Mainly Ourselves	Benefits Ourselves & Others

In my 12 years as a full-time pastor in two different churches, I offered pastoral leadership and care to hundreds of people. I remember vividly every funeral and wake I was part of, but one I remember more clearly than the others. I was used to conducting funeral services packed full of people, often with hundreds in attendance. These funerals became celebrations of the life and contributions of the one who had passed. Though there was sadness, there was also gratitude for the life lived and its contributions.

One funeral in particular stands out. It was in the town of Truro, Nova Scotia, on the Atlantic Coast of Canada. It is a smaller community, with decent, kind, and caring people. I was called by one of our local funeral homes to conduct a service for an older gentleman who had passed away. He had requested a minister preside at his funeral. Because I did not know him, I was unsure what to expect, but as I arrived, I was shocked to see an open casket, with one mourner in attendance. I checked my watch and made sure I wasn't early. Actually, I was five minutes late. I decided to wait another 10 minutes to see if anyone else would arrive. At 11:15am, 15 minutes after the funeral was supposed to begin, there was one mourner, an open casket, and myself present to celebrate and remember a life of more than 70 years.

I went through the motions of the funeral service, but was forever shaken by that experience. I couldn't imagine living 70 years, and connecting with so few people and touching so few lives that there would be only one attendee at my funeral, along with a paid minister. That event shook me to my core and I resolved that I wanted to build a *Temple* and not a *Tent* with my life. I have not lived a perfect life by anyone's estimation, but my heart and my aim has been to build a *Temple*-based life, benefiting others, not just living for *today* and for *myself*, but for *tomorrow* and for *others*. There can be no doubt that I will *Manage The Moments* more effectively if I spend my time building a *Temple*, as opposed to a *Tent*.

6) *We Must Make The Most Of Our Time*

This point is the next step in our natural progression. If all the time given to me is a gift, and if it is a tangible and a valuable resource, and I only have a limited amount of time, and if that time passes more quickly than I think, then I need to make the most of the time allocated to me.

A person who *Gets Where They Need To Go* and who **Lives Their LIFEFIT** is a person who makes the most of every moment of their Time. They are not *time wasters*, but *Manage The Moments* effectively and prudently. Peter Drucker said, *"Time is the scarcest resource and unless it is managed nothing else can be managed"*. He was saying that if we do not take the Time to manage our Time, then taking Time to manage anything else is a waste of Time. Try saying that 5 times in a row quickly!

So many times, as a Life & Business Coach, and as a Counsellor, people have said to me over the years: "I just don't have enough time to_____". You fill in the blanks, but it is all connected to their dream – write a book, finish their education, open a women's shelter, help the homeless, produce a play, design fashion accessories, etc.

"I just don't have enough time..." Well, as harsh as it sounds, here is the reality: *"Don't say you don't have enough time. You have exactly the same number of hours per day that were given to Helen Keller, Pasteur, Michaelangelo, Mother Teresea, Leonardo da Vinci, Thomas Jefferson, and Albert Einstein."*[57] Wow! *Managing The Moments* is making the most of the time you do have.

7) *We Value Our Time When We Value Ourselves!*

Lastly, *Managing The Moments* is all about self-worth. For me, one day this really sank in. People who do not value their own time do not really value their own selves. Until you value yourself, you will not value your time. People struggle with time management because they struggle to see their strengths, their talents, their gifts, their abilities, and the worth of what they have to offer. Until you value yourself and all you have to give, you will not value your time. *Managing The Moments* could be simplified into this: Seeing yourself and the beauty of all you have to offer, and placing such a high value on it that you do not waste a single **moment**. This is ***Managing The Moments***.

The Top 4 Time Management Tools

1. *Clarify Your Priorities*

The key to effectively *Managing The Moments* is right priorities. Right priorities are the key to life. There is a quote by

---

[57] H. Jackson Brown, Jr., 2000, *Life's Little Instruction Book*, Thomas Nelson Publishers, Nashville, TN

Johann Wolfgang Von Goethe that expresses this well: *"Things which matter most must never be at the mercy of things which matter least."*

Benjamin Franklin advised, *"Resolve to perform what you ought; perform without fail what you resolve."* In other words, we need to take time to clarify and determine our priorities, and then deliver on them. Clarify and determine your priorities, and then simply follow through.

People who have the right priorities in life don't have a problem in *Managing The Moments*. They cut through the distractions, the clutter, and the peripheral, and establish the right priorities by practicing the principle of *"Planned Neglect"*: planning to neglect *everything* that is not connected to their priorities and only doing that which is their priority. As Stephen Covey said: *"...You have to decide what your highest priorities are and have the courage — pleasantly, smilingly, non-apologetically, to say "no" to other things. And the way you do that is by having a bigger "yes" burning inside. The enemy of the "best" is often the "good."*[58]

What Are Healthy Priorities?

1. *Living According To My Values*

2. *Living According To My LIFEFIT*

3. *Giving Key Consideration To Family & Relationships*

4. *Paying Attention To The Things That Earn My Income*

5. *Focusing On Personal Growth Time*

6. *Ensuring Some Time For Personal Recreation*

---

[58] Stephen R. Covey. 1989. The Seven Habits Of Highly Effective People. New York, N.Y. Free Press, p.156,157.

2. Put Your Time On A Budget

In learning to *Managing The Moments,* we need to place an actual value on our use of Time and the activities that we engage in. Lee Iacocca said, "If you want to make good use of your time, you've got to know what's most important and then give it all you've got". Here are a few keys:

See Your Time As A "Fixed Income" – A "fixed income" is a salary. It is predictable. We need to see our Time in much the same way. We all have an uncertain allotment of Time given to us. Percy Whiting said it like this: *"Time is a fixed income, and as with any income, the real problem facing us is to how work successfully with our daily allotment. Plan each day down to the moment because once time is wasted, you can never get it back".* We are all on a *"fixed income"* of Time.

Follow Through On Your Priorities – Now that you have set your priorities, follow through on them. Live out what you have decided to keep and what to you have decided to cut. Determine to *"spend"* your Time so you get maximum value out of it! Jonathan Edwards said, *"I resolve to live with all my might while I do live. I resolve never to lose one moment of time and to improve my use of time in the most profitable way I possibly can. I resolve never to do anything I wouldn't do, if it were the last hour of my life".*

Design A Schedule – A schedule takes our *"vision"* of *Managing The Moments* and makes it realistic. How do we DESIGN A SCHEDULE?

- *Use Some Helpful Tools* – There is an abundance of tools available to us: day-timers, calendars, Microsoft Outlook; even most smart phones and mobile phones have some kind of time management tool.

- *Design A Schedule For Each Day* - Create a daily schedule to ensure that we live out our priorities.

- *Design A Schedule For Each Week* - Create a weekly schedule.

- *Design A Schedule For Each Month* - Create a monthly schedule.

- *Schedule In Non-Negotiable Essentials* – The essentials that you have no control over. You can basically fit school and work into this category, those commitments you cannot be flexible with.

- *Schedule In Negotiable Essentials* – These are essentials that you have control over, and some flexibility. You can basically fit the following here: exercise time, certain work commitments, key relationship time.

- *Schedule In Non-Negotiable Non-Essentials* – These are the non-essentials you have no control over. They are not flexible, but also are not essential.

- *Schedule In Negotiable Non-Essentials* – These are the non-essentials that you have control over, so you can be entirely flexible here.

- *Be Flexible* - In other words, don't be incredibly rigid. Roll with it!

3. Enhance Your Ability To Say No

To overextend yourself is to simply take on things that are not connected to your priorities. We need to be ruthless when we, or others (friends, opportunities, recreation, etc.) bring up things that are not in line with our priorities. This involves developing the ability to say no. We burn out when we overextend ourselves. Often the cure is as simple as a polite, *"No, thank you."* I love the quote by Lin Yu Tang: *"Besides the noble art of getting things done, there is the noble art of leaving things undone. The wisdom of life consists in the elimination of nonessentials."* This is *Managing The Moments!*

4. Take Time For Yourself

Take time for personal growth, recreation, exercise, rest and fun. Your joy is your strength, so when you lose your joy, you lose your strength. We need joy to be strong. We receive joy when we take the time we need for ourselves to revive, rejuvenate and rest. Learn to take time for yourself. This is all about *personal renewal…*

Personal Renewal:

☺ **For Rest** – Physical health. We must take time simply to rest and get our strength back. Proper amounts of sleep are crucial.

☺ **For Regular Exercise** – Physical health. Medical science has proven over and over again that physical, mental, emotional, and physiological health is tied to regular exercise. Make time for this.

☺ **For Relaxation** – Emotional Health. We need to learn what helps us relax, and what helps us to spend time in laughter. Laughter is necessary for health.

☺ **For Relationships** – Emotional Health. Take time to build the important relationships in your life and to keep them strong! If you do, the effect will be positive.

☺ **For Retreats** – Mental & Spiritual Health. Take time for Personal Retreats, mini get-aways. An amazing thing happens when we pause and cease to be still: Our mind is enlightened. Answers and solutions present themselves. The complex becomes simple. Our soul, like a tender plant, or even an infant child, needs to be continually nourished and cultivated. The power of a nourished soul is such that when properly nourished, we have the motivation, strength, and capacity to nourish and feed others. Personal Retreats are an incredible opportunity to withdraw from the hustle and bustle of daily life, so that our vision can again become clear, and so that the dust can be wiped away. Ovid, who lived way back from 43 B.C. to 17 A.D., said: *"Take rest; a field that has rested gives a bountiful crop."* You and I were born to yield a bountiful crop! This bountiful crop grows as we take time to rest and renew. Taking time for Personal Retreats is an important part of rest and renewal. Constantly feed yourself spiritually. Devote a tithe, 10% of your waking hours to taking time to feed yourself spiritually in a way that works for you.

In this chapter, we have taken a close look at some Truths About Time and The Top 4 Time Management Tools. We are transitioning to the "How". If I am clear about *Why I Am Here* and *Where I Need To Go*, the next question is *How Do I Get There?* We *Get Where We Need To Go* by **Managing The Moments** and using our time wisely. Time is our most valuable possession, and the details of how we *Manage Our Moments* will determine if we **Live Our** **LIFEFIT** or not. Time management, in the end, is a simple choice. It is not easy or without cost, but in the end, is do-able for all of us. We either *Manage The Moments,* or the Moments Manage us! Getting Where We Need To Go is about *Managing The Moments,* until we have no moments left.

Getting Where You Need To Go
Chapter 13 – Getting There:
Coaching & Mentoring

When I step back and take a look at how I have been able to *Get Where I Need To Go*, it is clear to me that my life has been shaped and sharpened by *Coaches and Mentors*. *Coaches and Mentors* have been absolutely crucial in partnering with me to help me *Live My* **LIFEFIT** and close the gap between my potential and my performance. *Coaches and Mentors* have helped narrow the distance between my actual daily life and the dreams in my heart.

As a young man, in essence, I grew up without a dad, and so early on I was drawn to those with a heart to *Coach and Mentor* others. I think I also instinctively understood there was a significant distance between my current location and where I felt I could go. There was a considerable space between what I felt I was capable of, and what I was currently achieving. There was room between my future potential and my current performance, and so I was intuitively drawn to those who could help me close this gap.

I guess early on I realized I would never be able to maximize my own potential and my possibilities without *Coaching and Mentoring*. Actually, I believe this is true for all of us. We will never maximize our potential in any area without coaching. It is not possible. You may be good. You may be *really* good. You may even be better than everyone else. But without outside input, without *Coaching and Mentoring*, you will never be as good as you could be. We all do better when somebody is providing feedback and input.

As a 16-year old, I was drawn initially to a leader named Evan. Evan was an influential person in the youth group I was a part of at the time. He was a caring and open individual who loved to have fun. He was also very grounded, and every time I was around him, I felt as though I was valuable and important. At that point in my life, I think I was crying out for someone to affirm me, to validate that who and what I was, was okay. I had started to get pretty deeply involved with drugs and alcohol, searching desperately to find a sense of myself, and Evan was the right person at the right time. He validated and affirmed that I was okay as I was, and helped me find myself without falling back on booze and drugs. Though he offered some guidance, he seemed to focus more on strengthening my sense of identity and personal worth. In a healthy and selfless context, Evan helped *me* to feel good about *me*, and this changed my life. I look back now and realize what an authentic *Coach and Mentor* Evan was to me, and I am grateful. Great *Coaches and Mentors* build our sense of self-worth and our sense of ourselves. They validate and affirm us.

Bruce came along a little later. Bruce was the kind of guy for whom you felt an instant respect and admiration. He had pulled himself up from very little to a place of pretty significant success, and was the sort of person of whom you might affectionately say: *"He did not suffer fools gladly"*. In other words, he wouldn't put up with my excuses and reasons for not following through and living up to the goals and standards I had set for myself. He would cut through the explanations and justifications I was so good at offering, and simply hold me accountable.

On more than one occasion, I remember him calling me out for not following through on my stated goals and objectives. At this time I was all about making grand declarations about where I was going, and how I was going to get there, and how amazing everything would be when I finally arrived. I had a keen desire to spell out, to anyone who would listen, all the things I wanted to do and how great it would be when I did them. Bruce, though he would listen intently and believed in me 100%, would carefully point out the contradictions between my stated goals and how I was living at that moment. He was aware of the disconnect between my actions and where I wanted to go, and was not shy to call me on it. He challenged me to wage war against personal passivity and to make the required changes. If I was actually going to move towards my intended destination, Bruce was clear that my actions today would determine my tomorrows. Though at times it was difficult to hear, I admired the fact he cared so much that he would challenge and even confront me, holding me accountable and answerable to my own goals and dreams. Great *Coaches and*

Mentors are courageous, see through the clutter, and hold us accountable.

Pastor Ted was the next significant *Coach and Mentor* in my life. He was the leader of the large and active church congregation I was part of at the time, and had a long and significant track record of leaving a positive footprint in the lives of others. His character, integrity, and skill in leadership stand out to me the most, along with his genuine care and concern. I was a young man at the time, fairly insignificant, and I was certainly not an important person in the congregation. One day I went to see him, and ask if we could meet on a monthly basis so I could pick his brain. Without any hesitation at all about busy schedules or all the demands on his time, he agreed, and we began to meet.

These were unstructured and relatively informal sessions, where I would simply sit with him in his office and ask him questions; questions about life, relationships, leadership, and spirituality. These conversations became key influencers for me in shaping my worldview and perspectives. He always saw the potential in me, and was careful to draw it out. But he combined that with a sense of realism and taking action in the present to determine outcomes tomorrow. Once again, he affirmed me for who I was, and validated my worth.

We lost touch for several years, because of geographical moves on my part, but reconnected about 13-14 years later. During our disconnection, I had gone through a roller-coaster ride of starting a family, establishing myself on my own career path and life direction, building some significant achievements and influence, and then seeing much of it crash down because of personal failure on my part. I was not really prepared to handle success. When we re-connected, I was very much still in re-building and restoration mode. He reached out to me with unconditional love and a heart of care. He continued to affirm and validate who and what I was, and offered me support and guidance as I continued my journey. Great *Coaches and Mentors* take time for us, validate us, and continue to stand with us when others don't.

In the time between my first interaction with Pastor Ted and our re-connection, I was gifted with a husband and wife couple who were significant *Coaches and Mentors* in my life, named George and Hazel. Actually, from a pure learning and leadership development standpoint, this couple may have left the largest footprint of all. They came into my life at the right moment for the right reasons.

This couple were the prototypical possibility-thinking, destiny-enhancing, opportunity-taking, dream-pursuing type of people. They continually saw my potential and believed I could hit it, and took the time and made the effort to stoke my passion around my possibilities, and help me get there. I treasured our times together and the moments I was given to glean from their wisdom and learning, and am eternally grateful to them. They taught me effective communication, public speaking, leadership, and team-building. They taught me about organizational behaviour, team leadership, building a culture, leading by vision, delegation, non-profit management, and developing the potential of others.

At that time, I was a key leader in our organization and they were the founders. At times, I saw other leaders who wouldn't allow themselves to be *Coached* or *Mentored* by them. In the realm of leadership, we sometimes operate under the misguided thought process that because we are leaders, we don't need to be led. We have a tendency to measure ourselves by the people around us, or even against the people we lead. They become our reference point. However, a great coach will measure your performance against your own potential. A coach helps you measure your performance against your own strengths, potential, and **LIFEFIT**, instead of against someone else's.

I would not be the same person, coach or leader without the contributions of this amazing husband and wife team to my life. Just by being around them, my life was transformed because they provided a clear model and example that I wanted to follow. Great *Coaches* and *Mentors* add value to us and enhance our contributions to the world, by simply being themselves.

Shortly after the gift of this amazing couple, I transitioned from the non-profit world to the rough and tumble world of high-level business management, in the for-profit world. Moving from the charitable sector to the *"not so charitable"* sector, was not a huge leap for me in terms of attitude, thinking, or perspective, because I was always entrepreneurial and business-minded in my approach. However, without the disciplines of millions of dollars on the line, shareholders, boards of directors, the pressure of delivering consistent profit, and efficiency-based management, I was not refined in my approach. I needed growth in the realms of structure, organization, leading teams, and business. I needed to get a little leaner, and sometimes even a little meaner.

At this time, the person I directly reported to in the business world stepped in and became my next *Coach and Mentor*. I'm not sure if Jason would ever describe himself as a *Coach and Mentor* to me, but in this transition in my professional life, he definitely was. He could see some of my strengths in terms of people skills, communication, and leadership. But, he could also clearly see my weak spots from a business perspective, in terms of structure, discipline, policy and procedure, execution, and attaining company objectives. He helped me to understand that in a business capacity, being liked wasn't always an option, and that in management our primary task was to execute objectives and deliver results. He definitely shaped my ability to think in terms of strategic realities, producing pre-determined standards, delivering profit, and enhancing company market share and position. Great *Coaches and Mentors* help get us there by pushing us above and beyond our current location. Great *Coaches and Mentors* are successful if they move us from where we are to where we can be.

Right around this time, another *Coach and Mentor* came into my life. As I was transitioning into business, I was also transitioning from a counselling role into a coaching role. I did a fair amount of research on different options for being trained and Certified for Life and Business Coaching. After extensive research, I settled on the Certified Coaches Federation. I loved the fact that they placed a high value on my professional experience, my life experience, and education. I enrolled in their program, and went through their training process. After taking the first level to be Certified as a Life and Business Coach, I continued to the next level, which is a Certified Master Coach Level. Then, I went a step further and became a Certified Master Coach Trainer, to be able to train and Certify others to coach. It was an amazing experience.

Along the way, not only did I gain this Certification and training, but I gained a *Coach and Mentor* myself. Derrick Sweet, the founder and President of the Certified Coaches Federation, became a personal *Coach and Mentor* for me as I made the transition to Coaching as a Profession, and continues to be all of that to this day. He continually sees the good in me, and pulls it out, fostering an open relationship of trust and accountability between us. When I need practical advice, strength and encouragement, or a listening ear, he is there. And he has helped enhance my abilities as a Coach, a Trainer, a business person, an entrepreneur, a writer, and a public speaker, in ways I never thought possible. Great *Coaches and Mentors* educate, they energize, they enable, they empower, and they enhance. Derrick has done all of that in my life, and more.

As I said earlier, my life has been shaped by *Coaches and Mentors*. *Coaches and Mentors* have been absolutely crucial in helping me ***Live My* LIFEFIT** and close the gap between my potential and my performance.

A critical point to remember is that there is no synergy on your own. Synergy is the energy released when two or more pool their strengths, resources, abilities, and talents, especially when the result is greater than the sum of their individual efforts. It takes at least two. I cannot create synergy on my own. Neither can you. When we partner with others, we add their value to our own lives. You are only as powerful as your ***Coaches and Mentors***.

Another key point here: teach-ability and having the mindset of a student is central to being *Coached and Mentored*. If you are not teachable, you are not Coachable. If you are not willing to learn, with humility and the ability to hear even hard truths at times, you cannot be Mentored. Andy Stanley put it like this: *"A good leadership coach will do everything in his power to close the gap between your potential and your performance. That may entail brutal honesty. Why? Because the painful truth is the fast track to increased performance.* "[59] So true! Many times in my own life I have discovered that the painful truth is the *"fast track"* to increased performance. I often ask myself if I want to take the *slow* track or the *fast* track to Getting Where I Need To Go. If I want the *fast* track, I need brutal honesty from my Coaches and Mentors. The *slow* track involves surrounding yourself with people too afraid to confront you with the truth about how your attitudes, actions and behaviours may be hindering you from *Getting Where You Need To Go.*

Most of the time, it is not what a coach *knows* or even can *do* herself that makes her valuable. It's what a Coach or Mentor *sees* that counts. That's why top Olympic and pro athletes pay professional coaches to coach them. The coach is not necessarily more knowledgeable or better at the sport than the one they're coaching. However, they are able to lend perspective to the performance of the athlete. By watching the athlete in action, working away at their craft, they can offer some outside observation and perception. This invaluable information can lead to subtle or sometimes dramatic changes in actions and behaviours, thus enhancing outcomes, performance, and results.

Coaches and Mentors are critically important in our lives, and in our professional development. Researchers asked nearly 6000 researchers from 77 large companies one important question: *"What contributed most to your professional development over the course of your career?"* Have a look at some of their responses, and what they considered as *"absolutely essential"* or *"very important"* to their professional development:

- Informal coaching/feedback -73%
- Role models – 71%
- Being told their weaknesses and strengths – 71%
- Being mentored – 60%
- 360 Degree Feedback – 54% [60]

---

[59] Andy Stanley. 2000. *The Next Generation Leader*. Sisters, Oregon. Multnomah Publishers, Inc. p.122.
[60] Helen Handfield-Jones, "Grow Great Executives: Give Them Great Jobs," *Leader to Leader*, No.14 Fall 1999, p.12.

Over 50% of these executives rated *Coaches and Mentors* as *"absolutely essential"* or *"very important"* to their professional development. If people near the top, in executive roles, identify Coaches and Mentoring as important to Getting Them Where They Needed To Go, then it will also be important for the rest of us.

There is a growing conversation today about the field of Certified Life & Business Coaching, and its influence. This is a growing area which began in its modern form in the late 1970s, and is gradually gaining prominence. It has now spread worldwide. This relatively new profession is emerging because of a major shift in social parameters. In the last 30 or so years, themes such as health and wellness, spirituality, empowerment, self-worth issues, and holistic approaches to life, relationships, business, and the environment we live in, have become the norm. Change, self-help, and personal improvement has become the rule. Continuous personal development has become the *"in thing"*. In that context, we have looked for people to guide us on our journey towards becoming all we can be and reaching our personal fullness. Though the profession of Certified Life & Business Coaching is relatively new, gurus and mystics, teachers and sages, shamans and guides, advisers and role models, leaders and educators, priests and prophets, wise men and women have always been with us: Coaches and Mentors...

- Terry Fox Had A Coach,
- Muhammad Ali Had A Coach,
- Tiger Woods Has Had Several Coaches,
- Wayne Gretzky Had Several Coaches,
- Michael Jordan Had Several Coaches,
- Most Great Public Speakers & Authors Have Coaches,
- Even Luke Skywalker Had A Coach!
- 99.9% Of Successful People Have Coaches!

Now, although Certified Life & Business Coaching is clearly therapeutic in that its aim is to enhance an individual's performance or life experience, there are significant differences between Coaching and Therapy. Coaching is short term (often 3-

12 months) and is solution-focused. Coaching understands the client is able and functional, and focuses primarily on the present and future, and not so much the past. Certified Life & Business Coaching *is a results-orientated systematic process in which the coach facilitates performance enhancement and skills development, rather than treating dysfunction.* This difference means that a coach can be far more direct, focused, and challenging, and can hold their client responsible for their commitment to change to a greater degree than the therapist can.

Studies indicate that 90% of the participants in coaching relationships reported significant increases in their areas of focus. Several participants described immediate beneficial changes, and 95% cited the process as worthwhile. Coaching is now estimated to be a $5 billion/year in the U.S., and a $500 million/year business in Canada. Sixty per cent of North American companies use or have used an Executive Coach.

Coaching is the path that serious people take to reach their goals. It is a tool to have a *"purposeful relationship"*:

Coaches and Mentors CONNECT – They *listen deeply and non-judgmentally.* Many people have not really been listened to for a long time. By listening, *Coaches and Mentors* become a *safe harbour.* In the place of safety and trust, transparency comes. We feel validated and empowered to *Get Where We Need To Go.*

Coaches and Mentors COLLABORATE – As a result of *connecting* and deeply listening, *Coaches and Mentors* begin the process of locating exactly where we are at. It is difficult to help a person *Get Where They Need To Go* without locating exactly where they are now. Once *Coaches and Mentors* locate where we are at right now, and help us clarify our goals, they begin to collaborate with us to move us to our ultimate destination.

Coaches and Mentors CRAFT – Through their *collaboration,* *Coaches and Mentors* begin to work with us to craft a precise strategy for achieving goals and actualizing dreams. They help us process the *"How To's"*: our strategies, approaches, and plans. An abundant world awaits if we plan our goals, and then work our plan. Ken Blanchard said, *"I believe providing feedback is the most cost-effective strategy for improving performance and instilling satisfaction."* In other words, the feedback we receive through *Coaches and Mentors* helps us realize more abundance than we would have without coaching.

Coaches and Mentors CLARIFY – The difference between a lack of focus and focus is as great as the difference between a light bulb and a laser beam. One can throw out some light; the other can cut through steel. So many of us have so many great ideas and plans and hopes and dreams... a good *Coach and Mentor* helps us to drill down from the general to the specific, from the dream-able to the do-able, from what we want to have to what we can't live fully without. The answers to most people's challenges are within; and a good *Coach and Mentor* helps explore those possibilities and clarify those solutions.

Coaches and Mentors CARE – *Coaches and Mentors* do what they do because they *care for people*. They see the potential in us, our dreams and goals and ideas and business plans, and want to help us achieve it. *Coaches and Mentors* care enough to measure us against our potential, and the courage to challenge, empower, and confront us until we get there.

Coaches and Mentors CREATE MOMENTUM – Finally, coaching is all about *creating momentum*. Good *Coaches and Mentors* may help people feel better, but great *Coaches and Mentors create* movement, results and *momentum*. I love the quote from Steve Jobs, one of the founders of Apple: *"Be a yardstick of quality. Some people aren't used to an environment where excellence is expected."* Coaching establishes priorities and clarifies goals, and is all about creating results. Once priorities have been established and goals have been clarified, results, profit, and bottom line return can be created. Forward movement, return on investment, and profit is important.

Warren Buffet said, *"If you can tell me who your heroes are, I can tell you how you're going to turn out in life."* Who are your heroes? Authentically understanding this is crucial because they are your future.

If I am clear about *Why I Am Here* and *Where I Need To Go*, the natural next question is *How Do I Get There?* Here we have taken a close look at *Coaches and Mentors*. It will be difficult, if not impossible, to maximize your potential and possibilities without *Coaching and Mentoring*. We all do better when somebody is providing honest and caring feedback, perspective, and input. And we all do better when we have someone to lean on for support and accountability.

Getting Where You Need To Go
Conclusion –
Getting Unstuck

We are nearing the end of our journey together. More than anything, I hope this book has helped you *Get Where You Need To Go*, and to see your incredible worth and value to the world around you.

Success today has so many definitions and perspectives, and seems for some to be elusive. My cry is to help reframe success as not so much about what you *accumulate* and *accomplish*, but about how closely you come to *Getting Where You Need To Go*. There is a different tune playing within each of our souls... and *"success"* is how closely our lives align with and express that melody. Again, the words of Bono of U2, speak to us here: *"I judge where we are by how close I am to the melody I'm hearing in my head, and how close are we to what we can do as a band to realizing our potential."* [61] True success is playing close to the melody... it is realizing your personal potential and closing the gap between "the now" and "the then"... it is *Getting Where You Need To Go*. *Getting Where You Need To Go* is **Living Your LIFEFIT**:

L – Learning About Your **Passions**

I – Investigating Your **Personality**

F – Finding Out Your **Gifts** & **Abilities**

E – Exploring & Clarifying Your **Mission**

F – Facilitating & Developing **Marketable Skills**

I – Including **Networking** & **Relationships**

T– Taking **Opportunities** As They Arise

---

[61] Assayas, Michka, *Bono In Conversation With Michka Assayas,* The Berkley Publishing Group, New York, New York, 2005, p.41

Let's proactively engage life and *Get Where We Need To Go* by *Living Our* **LIFEFIT**. Each day is a new opportunity to step up and step out, and to align a little closer with *Getting Where We Need To Go*. Nothing empowers more than making daily choices to move forward. Why not start today?

"Sometimes, I Do Things Big"

One day, the family and I went for a drive. We all packed in the minivan for a short trip, probably to grab some groceries. As we drove down the road and navigated Calgary traffic on a bright and sunny day, we got into a playful conversation about who was the biggest and the strongest in the family.

Our son Joshua, who was 5 at the time, decided to declare to his 3-year old sister, his mother, and myself that he was the strongest. There was no doubt in his mind that if push came to shove, he could take on me, his mom, and his sister.

Of course, faced with this foolhardy statement of bravado, I piped up that dad was the toughest. I boldly declared that I was the oldest, the biggest, the strongest, and could easily prove that if needed. I was skilled, I was smart, and I could think on my feet in a tough situation.

Then mom chimed in. She advised all us she was a covert student of various martial arts. She knew some top secret moves. Besides, she was privy to some mysterious weak spots in all of us. She felt she was probably the biggest and the baddest in the car.

The only other person in the car was 3-year old Julianna Joy. Julianna was a pretty tough cookie, but seemed a lot better playing with dolls and doing unique works of art with crayons than she was at mortal combat. Just when we thought the issue was settled with mom's declaration of dominance, Julianna, the youngest and the smallest, declared in words I will never forget: *"Daddy, sometimes I do things big too! Sometimes, I do things big!"* We all burst into laughter and bestowed on Julianna the honour of being the strongest and biggest person in the family!

"Sometimes, I do things big!" To succeed in life and to *Get Where You Need To Go*, we need to have this sense of courage, confidence, and even bravado! We need to boldly step up to the world and to life, and those around us, and declare that we can do it, we can achieve it, we can nail it and *Get Where We Need To Go* and *Live Our* LIFEFIT. There will be times when no one else will believe in you, times when people look at you and only see the surface, just like when we in the van only saw the surface of a 3 year-old girl. In these times people may judge you, misjudge you, or de-value what you have to bring to the table, simply because they don't see the whole picture of all you are: your LIFEFIT. Don't worry about it or stress over it. Simply step up to the plate and declare, *"Sometimes, I do things big too!"* Declare this because sometimes, you do things big, like everyone else! Declare this because you believe in you. Every time we make a choice to *Live Our* LIFEFIT we're doing something really big! Do something big by simply *Getting Where You Need To Go* and *Living Your* LIFEFIT. Make it happen and get unstuck. You aren't trapped, unable to make any forward movement. You can get unstuck!

Action Keys For Getting Unstuck:

1) Rejoice... Over The Uniqueness Of Your *LIFEFIT*

Please, take a moment to celebrate your uniqueness! There is no one like you. You are custom-designed and one-of-a-kind. Celebrate who and what you are, along with what you are becoming and where you are going. Don't be modest when it comes to filling out this questionnaire. Ask what is really important to you, and what resonates within yourself about yourself:

Living My *LIFEFIT:*

<u>L</u> – *Learning About* Your **Passions** – My *Passions* Are:

_____

_____

<u>I</u> – *Investigating* Your **Personality** – My *Personality* Is:

_____

_____

<u>F</u> – *Finding Out* Your **Gifts & Abilities** – My *Gifts & Abilities* Are:_____

_____

_____

<u>E</u> – *Exploring* & Clarifying Your *Mission* – My *Mission* Is:

_____

_____

<u>F</u> – *Facilitating* & Developing *Marketable Skills* – My *Marketable Skills* Are:_____

_____

<u>I</u> – *Including Networking & Relationships* – My *Network* Is:

_____

_____

<u>T</u> – Taking <u>Opportunities</u> As They Arise – My Opportunities Are:_____

_____

2) Reflect... On The Possibilities Of Your *LIFEFIT*

Take a moment to reflect on the possibilities of what you can achieve, and who you can achieve it with. Remember that no goal is beyond your reach, so long as it aligns with your **LIFEFIT**. You have empowerment and secret strength in the areas of your **LIFEFIT**, when you walk in alignment with it.

This was something I learned when I began to take on large amounts of leadership and responsibility. I was still young. People would ask if it seemed like a lot to me. In all truth, at the time, before I really understood the concepts of **LIFEFIT**, I would answer that I always felt confident doing the things I was born to do. It felt like wearing a perfectly fitted pair of shoes. This is the confidence and congruence that flows when we live in alignment with our **LIFEFIT**. I realized that obstacles can't stop you. Problems can't stop you. Most of all, other people can't stop you. Only you can stop you if you are seeking to do the things you were born to do: your **LIFEFIT**. You are only limited by the scope of your **LIFEFIT**. To *Get Unstuck and Live Your* **LIFEFIT**, reflect on all the possibilities of your **LIFEFIT**.

3) Realize... Your Worth & Your Value

Our worth and our value are not determined by what we have or what we have done. And our past actions and achievements are not always accurate indicators of our future actions and potential. Make sure that you carry on a healthy *internal conversation* around your *self-worth* and *value*.

Our *internal conversation* can be described as the conversation you have internally around your thoughts, your beliefs, your worth, and your value. Some of us have been programmed with some negative internal conversation over the years, perhaps due to our upbringing or negative influences. This internal conversation may shape us in far more ways than we think.

Dr. Alfred Korzybski said: *"God may forgive you for your sins but your nervous system won't."* In other words, your subconscious mind remembers everything... and it does not distinguish between the real and imagined. Everything that has happened to you has been stored on your internal hard-drive... your subconscious memory.

We need to do an internal scan of our subconscious and conscious and root out the negative and unhealthy internal scripts, files, and programs. *When is the last time you did this?* Begin challenging your own assumptions and *internal conversation.* Your *internal conversation* is your window on the world. Scrub it off every once in a while, or the light won't come in. And make sure you maintain a high sense of worth and value. *To Get Unstuck* and **Live Your LIFEFIT**, realize your worth and value.

4) Read... What Will Feed Your *LIFEFIT*

Charles Jones said, *"You are the same today that you are going to be five years from now except for two things: the people with whom you associate and the books you read."* Ensure you are feeding your mind and spirit with influences that support your **LIFEFIT**. The reality is that you grow as much as you sow. *To Get Unstuck* and **Live Your LIFEFIT**, sow seeds into yourself that will feed your **LIFEFIT**.

5) Relate... To Those Who Support Your *LIFEFIT*

This next point flows right along with the last one. Sometimes we allow ourselves to get close to those who judge us and misjudge us. They don't see our potential but they certainly point out our problems. Rather than empowering us to **Live Our LIFEFIT**, they can be a negative voice of fear, failure, and discouragement. And sometimes they think they are helping.

Stay away from them! Find people who will support you as you pursue Living Your **LIFEFIT**. Why do we willingly put ourselves close to those who don't believe in us, don't see our potential and value, and even seek to tear us down? If you look for them, you will be led to the right people at the right time who will see your **LIFEFIT** and support you as you pursue it. And you can support them! *To Get Unstuck* and *Live Your* **LIFEFIT**, relate to those who empower and support you!

6) Rage... Against Mediocrity and Stagnation

Burning desire. Passion. Zeal. Fire. Anger. Rage. These can all be potent forces for change and personal growth within our lives. We cannot become what we need to be by remaining what we are. So it makes sense to rage against mediocrity and stagnation in our lives!

William Blake said, *"What is now proved was only once imagined."* [62] There was once a small motel in a small town in west Texas called the *"It'll Do Motel"*. A lot of people live their lives that way: *"It'll Do!.. Just Do What You Have To."* We live in a world where often *mediocrity* and *ordinary* and *average* and *middle of the road* and *run of the mill* and *commonplace* is rewarded. We live in an age where people often don't get inspired to be more than *mediocre* and *ordinary* and *average* and *common*, primarily because life will still reward them with survival if they do not. In other words, you can survive and even survive well at times by simply being *mediocre* and *average*, and so a lot of people think, why not? *But great men and women have never thought this way.* Martin Luther King Jr. said:

> *"Whatever your life's work, do it well. A man should do his job so well that the living, the dead, and the unborn could do it no better."*

See, the *"extraordinary"* can happen in your life if you let it: if you care more than others think is wise, risk more than others think is safe, dream more than others think is practical, and expect more than others think is possible. This is the exact opposite of complacency. Ordinary can be attained if you care *just* what others think is wise, risk *just* what others think is safe, dream *just* what

---

[62] Various Authors, *The Merriam Webster Dictionary Of Quotations* (Springfield, Massachusetts: Merriam-Webster Inc., 1992), p.215

others think is practical, and expect *just* what others think is possible: "IT'LL DO". But "ordinary" was never the plan for us! *To Get Unstuck and* **Live Your LIFEFIT**, rage against mediocrity, ordinary, normal, and stagnation!

7) Respond... To The World By Living Your *LIFEFIT*

When it comes to *Living Your* **LIFEFIT,** *just do it!* Daniel Taylor said, *"Freedom is useless if we don't exercise it as characters making choices. We are free to change the stories by which we live. Because we are genuine characters and not mere puppets, we can choose our defining stories. We can do so because we actively participate in the creation of our own stories. We are co-authors as well as characters. Few things are as encouraging as the realization that things can be different and that we have a role in making them so."*[63]

My world can change if I want it to! Today, in ways both small and large, I can begin to *Get Unstuck* and **Live My LIFEFIT.** Sometimes we just need to pull ourselves together and make changes now to *Get Where We Need To Go!* There is a song by U2 that speaks to this... *"Stuck In A Moment You Can't Get Out Of"*:

> *"You've got to get yourself together*
> *You've got stuck in a moment, and now you can't get out*
> *of it*
> *Don't say that later will be better*
> *Now you're stuck in a moment*
> *And you can't get out of it"*[64]

Are you stuck in a moment? Was there an event, a situation, a circumstance, a difficulty, even something that

[63] John Eldredge. 2001. *Wild At Heart*. Nashville, TN. Thomas Nelson Publishers.
[64] http://www.u2.com/discography/lyrics/lyric/song/126/

started out well, but now has brought you to a place of inactivity, trapped by inertia? Are you stuck in a place where you have no momentum and can't move forward?

Is it time to get yourself together? Time to overcome a hurt or heal a wound? Time to move past that unhealthy relationship or that season of depression? Time to sort your way through the discouragement, the distress, and even the despair so you can *Get Where You Need To Go* and *Live Your* **LIFEFIT?** If not now, when? And if not now, why not?

Why be a victim? And why blame others? And why wait for all the variables around you to change and perfectly line up before you get on with your destiny. Go after it!

J.C. Penney said, *"No one need live a minute longer as he is, because the Creator endowed us with the ability to change ourselves."* We have the ability to change ourselves! *To Get Unstuck* and *Live Your* **LIFEFIT**, just do it! Today I am who I am, and I am what I am, because of who and what I have allowed to inhabit my interior world. We all have a goal box and a container, housing all the choices we choose to make. At this very moment I am WHO I am and WHERE I am because of what I've allowed to inhabit my goal-box and my container of choices. *I am where I am, not because of what has happened to me, but because of how I have responded to what has happened to me.* Respond to everything the world throws at you by choosing, day in and day out, to *Live Your* **LIFEFIT**. Now is the time.

In closing, John D. Rockefeller said: *"The road to happiness lies in two simple principles: find what it is that interests you…and when you find it, put your whole soul into it – every bit of energy and natural ability you have."* Put your whole soul into it! *Getting Where You Need To Go* and *Living Your* **LIFEFIT** deserves our whole soul. Now is the time to pursue this journey that never really quite ends. Peace.

About the Author

Abe Brown, M.R.Ed./C., Certified Master Coach

4 Key Things You Should Know About Abe Brown:

1) *Founder and President of Momentum Coaching.* (2007 to present). Momentum Coaching has experienced 125% growth each year for the last four years. Abe has trained over 600 Life and Business Coaches right across Canada and the USA. He has mentored both Life and Business Coaches from more than 5 major Coaching Industry associations including the Certified Coaches Federation, the International Coaches Federation, Coach University, and others. He has delivered keynote speeches, motivational talks, and conducted seminars and workshops all over Canada and the USA. He wrote *Getting Where You Need To Go*, which is selling worldwide, and has developed life and business coaching tools which have been put into use all over North America and the world.

2) *Experienced Business Leader and Manager.* Abe has successfully turned around several failing businesses to the tune of millions of dollars, time and time again. This involved applying solutions to multiple issues such as driving sales growth, facilitating human resource management, expediting human capital maximization, empowering full employee engagement, and executing strategic direction, brand management, marketing, inventory management, and loss prevention. He has led businesses up to $25 million in annual revenue and up to 200 employees. He has increased profit margin, decreased loss, minimized inefficiency, and eliminated lack of synergy and rhythm.

3) *Non-Profit Leader, Educator, Administrator and Counsellor.* (1993 to present). Abe pastored several churches that experienced consistent year over year growth rates of 300%

or more, led a post-secondary educational institution with over 100 full-time students and satellites in 12 countries, and spent over 15 years as a counsellor, coach and personal growth specialist. He has spoken to crowds of a handful up to several thousand, and conducted trainings, workshops, and break-out sessions in educational, governmental, non-profit and business organizations. He received the *International Coach of the Year Award* in 2010 and 2011 from the Certified Coaches Federation. Abe is the President of the Certified Coaches Federation –
www.certifiedcoachesfederation.com

4) *Devoted Family Man and Hobbyist.* (1999 to Present). He is happily devoted to his wife, Euniz, and his two children, Joshua and Julianna Joy. A voracious reader of titles on business leadership and management, non-profit challenges, sociology, different cultures, emerging economies, investing, real estate, politics, economics, theology, philosophy, and spirituality. Avid composer and music lover. Lover of photography and the integration of video in an HDSLR format. Enjoys running, the odd party and celebration, karaoke, and healthy eating!

Call or email for more info today! 403-389-1190
abe@momentumcoach.ca
www.momentumcoaching.ca

CPSIA information can be obtained
at www.ICGtesting.com
Printed in the USA
LVOW12s1717010416
481782LV00001B/42/P